Keith Hill is a New Zealand writer whose work explores the overlap between mysticism, history, science, religion and psychology. His books include *The God Revolution, Striving To Be Human,* and *Practical Spirituality,* each of which won the Ashton Wylie Award, New Zealand's premiere prize for spiritual writing. He is currently investigating contemporary developments in mysticism.

Reviews of *The God Revolution*

"Hill's exposition is a fine example of scrupulously rigorous scholarship – it is remarkable how much ground is covered within his brief historical survey. ... An impressive and accessible introduction to a challenging philosophical topic. " – Kirkus Review

"Keith Hill is a writer in the vein of Karen Armstrong ... The prize that celebrates New Zealand's forward thinkers is thoroughly deserved."
– Mike Alexander, Sunday Star Times

"A scholarly yet accessible book. ... Deserves to be read by all those who care about ideas, the trajectory of civilization and its future form."
– Peter Dornauf, www.eyecontact.com

EXPERIMENTAL SPIRITUALITY

Keith Hill

attar books

Copyright © Keith Hill 2013
ISBN 978-0-473-25667-8
Cover designed by Abigail Kerr
First published by Attar Books 2013

Attar Books
www.attarbooks.com

CONTENTS

The Arousing Of Thought

W E HERE ANNOUNCE THIS as the start of a series of five books that deal with aspects of spirituality for contemporary seekers. By "we" is meant a nonembodied spiritual entity that has lived a cycle of lives on this planet and is now intent on sharing, from the spiritual domain, what it has learnt. Thus this book, and those that follow, are channelled literature.

The reason we are undertaking this series is that there is an urgent need today to promote spirituality and spiritual exploration outside the restrictions of religion. We say restrictions because religions carry the baggage of, in many cases, thousands of years of assumptions regarding the nature of reality, how the world came to be, and how human beings should be in it.

Religiously generated baggage includes the innumerable and often contradictory ideas people have about such things as what God is, God's relationship to humanity, the moral values human beings should live by, how the spiritual dimension relates to the physical dimension, and the nature of human identity, especially the relationship between human physical embodied identity and human spiritual non-embodied identity.

The problem with this religious baggage is that it obscures the vision of those who wish to enquire into their spiritual nature. It is not that all traditional religious ideas are wrong and invalid. The problem is that valid and invalid concepts are intermixed and are given equal weight by those who are unthinkingly involved in religion. This problem is further exacerbated when religious leaders expound a mixed package of beliefs and expect believers to gulp them all down.

Religions have flourished historically because in fact many people are quite happy to gulp down what is fed them, whether due to fear, a desire for comfort, or laziness. The fear is of being ostracized by the community in which they live, desired comfort is the ease of life that results from surrendering to others' authority, and laziness results because many don't want to make the effort to work things out for themselves.

On the other hand many others, and we are still talking historically, have found being a religious believer a decidedly uneasy, even unhappy, experience. This is because religions involve a hierarchy in which ordinary believers are expected to follow the lead of their supposed spiritual superiors and to surrender to them their volition and capability of feeling, thinking and acting as independent spiritual beings. This is how the religious requirement to surrender one's volition to one's supposed betters simultaneously generates happiness and unhappiness – happiness among those who want to surrender themselves, unhappiness among those who innately feel they should not surrender their ability to choose.

A significant consequence of being brought up in religious beliefs is that thinking individuals are required to accept many ideas that are not only contrary to what is generally accepted as known about the world and that offend plain common sense, but are also, and this is even more significant, contrary to what they inwardly feel about the world. We could call this feeling their personal spiritual sense, in contrast to collective conditioned prejudice and ignorance. This is why religiously generated package deals of beliefs need to be challenged by anyone who seeks deeper understanding. And, in fact, even many committed believers *do* challenge them in their own quiet way. How can this be?

Officially, Christian believers are required to accept all the teachings and beliefs promulgated by their religious elders, and not pick and choose from among them. Of course, in reality, and unofficially, most believers do discretely pick and choose to a greater or lesser degree. This happens across all religions, where some absurd ideas are rejected by the mass of believers, even if the doctrine continues to be preached officially. Recent surveys have shown that only a minority of Christians today believe in hell as a literal place, or accept that Mary ascended into heaven in her physical body. The

Catholic Church's forbidding of birth control is also accepted by a decreasing number of believers.

How is this diversity of beliefs allowed within religions? By the simple expedient of people not discussing what they truly believe. If no one asks a worshipper about their personal beliefs then they don't have to lie or respond in a way that is awkward for all. In this way connived silence allows a diverse collection of believers to worship together, with everyone content that their variously shaded misconceptions, truths and untruths won't be confronted.

Of course, the most effective way of choosing valid concepts about the world and rejecting the invalid is, even if only temporarily, to step outside the strictures of religion altogether. In this way you can survey your options without being obliged to contend with ideas that make no sense in the context of contemporary knowledge, or that personally offend you morally, metaphysically or spiritually.

Ideas such as that souls will go to hell if they don't believe in God or if they make the wrong life choices, that good people go to heaven for obeying their God, and that fealty to one's spiritual betters is required in order to prove obedience, are grounded in ancient notions that each individual has a particular place in a supposed spiritual hierarchy and has to obey the rules. These hierarchies and rules are not only outmoded today, they provide a significant portion of the baggage that enquirers need to jettison in order to obtain at least a minimal degree of clarity about the nature and purpose of their existence as spiritual beings.

This is why we begin this book by asserting that those who wish to explore their spiritual possibilities – possibilities that exist not far away, in another time or dimension, but are in fact intimately close, being woven into the very texture of everyone's daily existence – need to step outside the restrictions religions place on them and examine not just the world but also their lives with fresh eyes and untainted heart and mind.

However, one caveat has to be made to this assertion. It reflects the difficulty of making sweeping statements that apply to each and every individual in each and every circumstance. It must be acknowledged that the broad points being made here need to be evaluated in the light of specific cases and scenarios. Doing so leads to the following caveat to the previous paragraph.

RELIGIOUS COMMITMENT AND SPIRITUALITY

Numerous individuals have a life task that involves wrestling with a self-chosen religion in one of three ways. For some, being converted to a religion is a necessary phase in their inner development, because they need that religion's structures and strictures in order to turn their life around and give their life journey stability and direction. The fact that they are also embracing numerous errors is just part of the experience, providing materials they will need to extract themselves from at an appropriate later time.

For others, a significant part of their life journey, especially during their teen and early adult years, involves the process of extracting themselves from the faith they were raised in and overcoming their religious conditioning. The process of extraction provides them with an excellent opportunity to think things through for themselves and to develop their own perspective on the world and how they should live – for all religions do contain valid and positive concepts and values that may usefully be wrestled free from the jumble of morals, attitudes and ideas inculcated into them from birth.

A third group consists of those who can clearly see the many limitations and errors present in the religion they subscribe to, but instead of walking away they accept the challenge of staying and working to update the religion from within. For these individuals the often apparently thankless task of winnowing the chaff from the wheat is a service they take on to help their fellow believers who are more bound in their outlooks. In the process they, as do the other two categories of those involved in religion, have an excellent opportunity to work on further transforming themselves internally.

Of course, excluded from this self-transformative process are those who use religion to dominate, cower, punish or even torture others. The word "torture" is appropriate here because while the Inquisition no longer openly breaks bones and tears and sears flesh, nonetheless there are many psychological ways that religious dogmas continue to be used to torture believers physically, emotionally and mentally.

We also acknowledge that those who possess a streak of power or dominance do not need religion to torture others. They do perfectly well in crime, business, politics, justice, education or the many other careers that place one individual above others and so provide an opportunity that proves too tempting for those who are psychologically predisposed to oppress and hurt their fellow beings.

AN EXAMPLE OF RELIGIOUS CONDITIONING

Restrictions not only come from outside one's sensibility, in the form of erroneous assumptions about the world, but just as importantly, and perhaps even more so, from within one's own sensibility.

Restrictions, errors and baggage are buried deep within each individual's psychological make-up. However, individuals rarely clearly perceive their own deeply buried inner baggage until they have first thrown off their externally conditioned baggage. And as has been repeated, much of that external baggage is provided by religious beliefs.

To be more specific about how this process occurs, let's take the example of religiously-conditioned guilt. Let's say a woman responds to an inner urge to explore her own spiritual nature – very likely this is why you, the reader, have picked up this book in the first place. However, this enquiring woman has been brought up in the belief that she was born sinful. This belief was inculcated into her from childhood, via her local church and reinforced by her parents who automatically repeated what they themselves were told during their own childhood.

So while, on the one hand, this enquiring woman wishes to investigate her spiritual nature, let's say by taking part in a meditation workshop, on the other hand she keeps being assailed by the thought that she is a sin-filled soul. Very likely, she feels guilty about stepping outside the activities of her church, having also been brought up to believe that her church's particular set of beliefs are superior to those of other churches. Or even that there is no salvation outside her church. Even worse, years of being inculcated with the idea she was born guilty of sin have established an inner psychological pattern of low self-esteem, maybe even to the extreme of feeling in her most down moments that she is utterly worthless.

The upshot is that she wishes to explore her spiritual possibilities, but conditioned guilt fills her with the assumption that she isn't worthy of such an enquiry, and that anyway she will almost certainly fail if she tries. In such a case, the woman's meditation will not be successful unless and until those guilt-instilled patterns of feeling and thinking are sufficiently diminished to allow an inner silence to be maintained. Full ongoing engagement with her spiritual core will not occur until those traits are eliminated.

In practice, what often happens is that when the meditation workshops attended by guilt-filled spiritual explorers do not provide immediate change, those enquirers give up that avenue of exploration and either return to being dominated by their conditioned worldview or, and this is reasonably common, they end up being embittered about both religion and spirituality.

And even if our enquirer does have a revelatory experience during the workshop, (assuming she manages to put aside her conditioned baggage long enough to connect to her spiritual self), afterwards her conditioned guilt-driven attitudes will surge back into place and likely overwhelm the memory of what she experienced. The result is that she at first doubts the validity of what she experienced, and then, over time, allows the memory of what she experienced to be buried by conditioned baggage. So while the impression of experiencing her own spiritual self cannot be lost, because it is retained within at a deep level, that impression doesn't feed her during her ongoing life in the way that it certainly could and should have.

What this example shows is that in order to explore one's spiritual nature one first has to slough off the religious, moral and metaphysical baggage that childhood conditioning, and sometimes adulthood conditioning, piles on top of most human beings to a greater or lesser degree.

The process of sloughing off the baggage is similar to building a house. First one has to clear the land on which the house is to be built. Only after obstructions are removed (assuming legal requirements have been satisfied and planning consent obtained) is it possible to start building one's new house. In the same way only after conditioning is addressed, physical, emotional and intellectual impediments removed, and one allows oneself to proceed, is it possible to seriously start building a new inner spiritualised sensibility.

Thus we reiterate: In order for individuals to have a clear and rational process for exploring their spiritual potential, there is a need today to advocate for spirituality outside the strictures and restrictions of religion. That task is addressed in these pages, this book being the first in a series of five that promote the task of spiritual exploration and development within a non-religious conceptual framework.

NON-RELIGIOUS SPIRITUAL EXPLORERS

Yet before proceeding we need to acknowledge that there is another class of individuals who are already drawn to engage with spirituality outside a religious context. This class consists of those who were raised in non-religious households and so were exposed to little, or even no, religious conditioning.

These households range from the irreligious, in the sense that religion in any form was simply ignored, to the agnostic, in which any of the many different forms of religious expression may have been acknowledged to a greater or lesser degree but with none being expressly adhered to, to the atheistic, in which a belief in God is not upheld, to the rational, whether philosophically or scientifically inclined, in which concepts drawn from current culture and knowledge are used to comprehend the world.

Individuals brought up in households in which non-religious outlooks were provided by their parents, or who embraced one of these perspectives during their teen or adult years, may or may not have been inculcated into a spiritual orientation of some kind. In fact, not having such an orientation is no impediment to their inner progress. This is because all human beings possess a spiritual core and not seeking to actively engage with that core does not mean that an individual is in any way a lesser spiritual being than someone who enquires into themselves. Because that is certainly not the case. Their life journey just has a different momentum to it, that is all.

However, we do acknowledge that those who do wish to consciously engage with their spiritual core, and who were brought up in or now live in non-religious households, often have an advantage over their religiously-raised cousins. This is because they have less baggage to overcome before they can begin exploring their inner depths. To return to the metaphor of building the house, in general their "land" has fewer obstructions on it, and so less effort is required to prepare the conditions necessary to begin building their "house" of refined inner spiritual sensibility. That is why, for those individuals, not having a religious upbringing can provide them with a distinct advantage when they decide to open themselves up to spiritual possibilities.

Yet there is one sub-class of individuals among those brought up in non-religious households for whom this advantage is not the case. We will identify them as those who uphold the scientistic outlook.

THE SCIENTISTIC OUTLOOK AND BEING CLOSED

The *scientistic outlook* needs to be separated from the *scientific method*. The scientific method involves using an experimental process to arrive at knowledge about the world. To describe this process perhaps over-simplistically, the sciences use existing data to modify an existing theory about the world or to generate a new theory altogether. An experiment is then designed to test the theory. The data derived from the experiment then either confirms, partially confirms, or denies the validity of the proposed theory. Where necessary the theory is adjusted, or a new theory proposed, and another experiment is designed to test it. This process is repeated until theory and experimentally derived data agree with each other. Old understanding is then transcended and new understanding established. Scientific progress occurs as a result of repeatedly questioning what is known in order to arrive at new understanding.

A scientific theory, then, is a proposal about something in the world that is always open to further refinement and to being adjusted so it more exactly reflects what is perceived and known. A practical outcome is that scientifically confirmed knowledge is used as foundations on which to build new technologies. For example, Maxwell's theories about light being electromagnetic in nature led to the discovery of x-rays which today are used in a wide range of practical applications, from medical examination to airline security. Thus the scientific method is an experimentally-oriented process in which existing data is questioned, a new theory is proposed to account for the data, the theory is tested experimentally, confirmed or further refined, and eventually new understanding is arrived at, understanding that is applied practically in the world.

In contrast, the *scientistic outlook* consists of a metaphysical view of the world. The term *scientistic* has various definitions. Here the scientistic outlook is defined as one in which reality is considered to be no other or more than the natural physical world. Commonly assumed by-products of the scientistic outlook are that only the material world exists, that there is no realm apart from or beyond the material world, that human consciousness is entirely a by-product of the biological and chemical processes of the body's central nervous system and its brain, that no non-material spiritual or supernatural entities such as God or gods or extra-natural powers exist, and that what cannot be explained in materialistic and naturalistic terms does not exist.

These by-products are all actually no more than assumed truths that this class of people choose to make. We call them "assumed truths" because they have not been arrived at via testing. If scientistically-inclined individuals applied the scientific method to their own assumptions about the world they would treat their assumptions as propositions, not as truths, and design experiments to test them. The result would be that, one by one, they could validate or invalidate their assumed truths.

Of course, this is not how those with a scientistic outlook approach the assumptions that underpin their outlook. While they may gleefully challenge and attack others' truths, especially the truths of the religiously inclined, they consider their own truths to be sacrosanct. Yet, ironically, here is where scientistic individuals and individuals firmly embedded in their religious beliefs may be categorised together. For neither is open to questioning the assumptions that underpin their worldviews. And so both categories equally shut themselves off from discovering fundamentally new knowledge about the world and about themselves.

Psychologically, scientistic and religious belief-sets each equally function as a lens or filter through which individuals view the world. The result is that any feeling, concept or information that doesn't accord with their assumptions is either deliberately or unconsciously coloured by them and made to conform, or is rejected outright. Accordingly, they only ever learn in relation to a narrow band of new perceptions, feelings or ideas that already exist within the strict limitations of their existing worldview.

Such individuals will only ever refine what they already know, and never open up for themselves what they don't know. In a psycho-spiritual sense, because they refuse to question the foundations on which their worldview rests, no fundamental inner transformation is possible.

MAKING THE IMPOSSIBLE POSSIBLE

The outlook behind this book is that fundamental transformations are not only possible, they are essential to experiencing, processing and learning new feelings, new thoughts, new ways to act, and making new choices.

To use a rhetorical device, only by first being prepared to entertain the possibility that the impossible is possible will the impossible in fact become possible. And by the term "impossible" is meant that which exists outside the framework of what you currently consider possible. For the truth is that no matter how much you have already experienced and know, there are always new experiences, and new concepts to contextualise those experiences, that assuredly will challenge your most fundamental assumptions about reality and your identity. There are always new experiences and knowledge that, if you encountered them, would bring crashing down everything you accept as fundamentally true about what you know and are.

This is a reflection of how vast reality is, of how many possibilities exist within reality, and of how little any embodied human being can possibly know about all that exists, given the limitations inherent in being a spiritual consciousness functioning within the constricted human sensory apparatus and its brain. For this is the ultimate limitation that afflicts human beings when they seek to discover what is occurring around them: they have only their human capacities to make order and meaning out of what they find.

In this sense it could be said that the scientistic and the conservative religious outlooks are actually defence mechanisms. They are ways of hiding from the full enormous breadth and depth of reality that, when considered from a limited human perspective, appears frightening in its vastness. The scientistic and conservative religious outlooks are ways of explaining away, or of justifying why one should ignore, the full wonder and mystery of all that is. Ultimately, all that is is a mystery. And the glory of existence is that there is always another experience to wonder at. There is always yet another mystery to enter into and explore.

Given that reality is brimming with mystery, everyone has two fundamental choices. One can choose to put up the shutters of one's house and
allow in only narrow squeaks of daylight, moonlight or starlight. Or one can
choose to be adventurous, throw the shutters wide, open oneself up, and
make oneself available to the possibilities inherent in what exists.

For wherever you are at any particular moment, during any particular
life, is only one portion of all the possibilities that exist on Earth, let alone of
all the possibilities that exist throughout all that is.

EXPERIMENTAL SPIRITUALITY

This book is not for the religious and scientistic who wish to remain behind
their shutters and hold tight to their cherished assumed truths about the
world and themselves. This book is for the adventurous who wish to learn
how to step out of their everyday selves in order to experience and understand what they have not yet experienced and have not previously known or
understood.

In order to help initiate such adventures, in order to facilitate new ways
of perceiving, feeling, thinking, choosing and acting, this book presents an experimental approach to spirituality. It proposes that whatever you have been
told, including what is stated in these pages, should be treated not as a truth,
but instead as nothing more than a proposition. And all propositions must
be tested in the cauldron of personal experience to ascertain whether they
reflect an unbiased and knowledgeable perception of reality. If, after testing,
it is found that a particular statement does reflect perceived reality, it can be
accepted as valid. Alternatively if, after testing, it does not reflect perceived
reality, then it may be rejected as invalid.

Any statement that is not validated via testing is open to being rejected.
But it may not be rejected until it *is* tested. Rejection on the basis of assumption, without testing, is ignorance. Rejection as a result of testing facilitates
separating the erroneous from the correct.

Of course, it is also the case that failure to validate propositions experimentally does not automatically mean they are incorrect. It may be that the
testing process is partial or faulty. And perceived reality itself is also open to

misinterpretation, even misperception. So all results need to be evaluated before being accepted or rejected. Repeated testing is one way to do this. Another is to check your results against what others in the same situation have discovered.

Testing propositions provides a way of arriving at experimentally validated knowledge. Any proposition that is validated through repeated testing via personal experience may be accepted as a truth. Some truths are personal truths, being valid for you but not necessarily applying to others. Social truths apply to the society in which you live. World truths apply to the wider world, which includes the Earth and its Milky Way Galaxy. Universal truths are truths that apply throughout reality.

But, of course, discovered truths have a way of being superseded by new truths. So any truth is in fact never anything more than a standing truth, a provisional truth, a truth which will do for now until new experiences reveal limitations in the premises or in the processes on which any currently accepted truth is established. Accordingly, everyone needs to constantly challenge their assumptions, test their truths' underlying premises, and be prepared to refine, discard or transcend what they know. As a result of evaluating the outcomes of testing, everyone will eventually arrive at new provisional truths. Which in their turn will be tested, challenged, refined, discarded or transcended. This process of continually refining accepted truths has no theoretical end, as long as we keep enquiring and questioning what we accept and know. In this way we forge onwards into the previously unknown. And we are able to claim from it new knowledge and understanding.

Over the past four hundred years human culture *en masse* has forged ahead remarkably in terms of new scientific knowledge and new technologies derived from that knowledge. Such progress has been possible because many individuals utilised the scientific method to question what was known and accepted as true. The result was that they uncovered not just the previously unknown, but the previously inconceivable. That inconceivable then became the new accepted known. And this new known was itself subsequently overturned as enquirers kept forging into yet newer unknowns. Which eventually surrendered their secrets and became a newly extended known. Containing, of course, a further unknown. And so on.

Experimental Spirituality aims to show spiritual enquirers how they may profitably question what they know of reality and of themselves, how they may uncover the unknown, and even the inconceivable, and how they may use their newly acquired knowledge and understanding to travel even further into the unknown. Because, of course, however much anyone knows, there is always more to be experienced, more to be explored, more to be learnt, more to be absorbed, and more to be understood.

Understanding is a light. Human beings are surrounded by the darkness of ignorance – given that human ignorance consists of a lack of knowledge of the reality in which they exist. Just as individual scientists, and small groups of scientists working together, have thrown light into the darkness to the benefit of all humanity, so individual spiritual enquirers, and small groups of such enquirers working together, may shine a light into the unknown that surrounds human awareness and make progress for the benefit of all.

This is a new century. It promises new knowledge and new possibilities. *Experimental Spirituality* offers fourteen propositions in order to contribute to the development of an experimental approach to spiritual exploration relevant to those living in the twenty-first century.

May these propositions help you ignite the lamp that you are. And may you cast light for the benefit of all!

FOUR PREMISES

CHAPTER 1

Unquestioned
Assumptions Are Limiting

H UMAN EXISTENCE IS BUILT on many assumptions, yet few people examine the assumptions that are most fundamental to their lives. This is because their assumptions are so integrated into daily perceptions that people
either remain unaware of their existence or, if they are aware, the thought of
examining their fundamental assumptions is so frightening that they choose
to ignore that possibility altogether.

Where do these assumptions come from? Most are conditioned by peers,
family and community. A significant part of growing up involves trying out
selected assumptions for size. During their teenage years everyone tests ideas
and attitudes through debating and reading, through hanging out with like-
minded and unlike-minded friends, by joining clubs or religious, political,
ecological, or artistic groups, or by adopting outlooks and behaviours that
directly challenge the views of parents and the authority of the immediate
community.

However, by their twenties most people have settled into the outlook
that they then maintain for the rest of their lives. Over subsequent years
the ways they express their outlook may change, resulting in a decision to
swap causes, religions, political outlook or allegiances. But the underlying
premises, the foundational values that they consider to be most important to
them, largely remain unchanged. As a result, following their formative teenage years very few individuals examine the assumptions they live by. And
whenever their assumptions are challenged by others they tend to be at a loss
as to how to justify what they accept and believe. So they fall back on bluster,

make emotional assertions, or refer to an authoritative person or a revered book (be it religious, political, economic or scientific) to justify what they assume to be the case about themselves and the world.

But if they stood back from all this bluster and were honest with themselves, they would see that really they have great difficulty proving the truthfulness and validity of most, if not all, of their fundamental assumptions. Instead, those assumptions are just there. So they sit in the great armchair of their outlook, which is firmly bolted to their assumptions, surveying others and making unquestioned pronouncements about the world's rights and wrongs from its cushioned comfort. Yet, and this is one of life's great ironies, the fact is that while on the one hand unexamined assumptions greatly limit one's perception of the world, on the other hand everyone certainly does need to make assumptions in order to live together in the world. How so?

HUMANITY'S NEED FOR ASSUMPTIONS

A community of people living together needs social and behavioural parameters that everyone signs up to in order to live together in an orderly fashion. Broadly speaking, these assumptions consist of traditional customs, social norms and legally established laws. However arbitrary or even wrong-headed these customs, norms and laws might be, they hold communities together.

Eventually, however, the question is asked: How fair, right or common sense are these? This question is initially asked by enquiring individuals who are uncomfortable with certain aspects of their community's social assumptions. It is only when injustices become glaring, because attention has been focused on them by those individuals, that communities as a whole start questioning the assumptions that underpin their interactions.

Given sufficient time human beings come to address and change assumptions that exploit, suppress or injure one class of people to the benefit of another class, replacing them with more equitable and nurturing laws, norms and customs. This is the way human communities and nations progress.

Exactly the same process occurs on the individual level. Each person has a number of ingrained assumptions about the world and about themselves that cause them to behave unfairly or harshly towards others. These behaviours, which are reinforced by negative attitudes, prejudices and biased thinking, not only cause them to impinge on others but, and this is arguably more significant, limit their ability to learn, develop and progress.

On the other hand, each individual does need to adopt a number of such assumptions, however right or wrong. Why? Because just as traditions, norms and laws hold a community or nation together, giving it social cohesion and identity, so the assumptions individuals make about themselves and others – however right or wrong, valid or invalid, nurturing or limiting they might be – hold together their personal identity. The fact is, without these basic assumptions individuals are lost, not knowing how they should think or act. Or, indeed, who they are.

We will have more to say about identity as an auto-construction shortly. For now it is sufficient to make the point that the assumptions people make about themselves, and equally about the world they live in, also underpin their identity. This is why, when people's assumptions are questioned or pricked, tempers flare and equanimity unravels – because they feel it is not just their assumptions that are being questioned, but their personal identity.

Accordingly, if you wish to explore your spiritual identity and achieve new knowledge and understanding, maintaining unquestioned assumptions and allowing them to tint your outlook is a huge limitation. In order to grow everyone needs, first, to acknowledge and confront the ingrained assumptions that rule their lives, second, sift the valid assumptions from the invalid, and third, replace invalid and limiting assumptions with assumptions that testing has transformed into useful knowledge.

Acknowledging, questioning and replacing assumptions with knowledge is a key challenge that everyone engaged in a spiritual quest needs to take up in order to progress in their journey of growth.

ASSUMPTIONS IN SCIENCE AND RELIGION

In the sciences, fundamental assumptions are called axioms. An example of a scientific axiom is that only empirical data provides valid information about the world. Another scientific axiom is that matter in the physical world has no inherent purpose, so whatever happens in the world occurs according to natural processes that are innate in it, and that interact according to biological drives or physical and sub-physical interactions. Chance also impacts on the way events are initiated, develop and play out in the world.

In religions, fundamental assumptions are grouped together to form a credo. Each religion has its own credo, which provides believers with the conceptual foundations for their beliefs. A belief fundamental to Christianity is that worthy believers will go to heaven after their body dies. The Dharmic religions (Hinduism, Buddhism, Sikhism and Jainism) have an equally fundamental belief in reincarnation. Most religions share the fundamental belief that supernatural beings, whether in the form of God, angels or saints, will answer prayers and help worshippers get through difficult times.

Of course, while religions and the sciences have collective credos and axioms, in practice many individual members of religious groups or scientific disciplines don't accept all that others in their groups or professions assume. They individualize their credos. Accordingly, some Christians assume the literal reality of angels and heaven and hell, while others do not. Similarly, some scientists assume that nothing other than the material universe exists, and that the universe has no purpose, while others do not. However, there is a significant difference between the attitude towards assumptions made by scientists and the religious.

For the religious, credos are not to be challenged or altered, because they provide the religion with its identity. Change the basic beliefs that underpin the credo and the religion is no longer itself. Psychologically, there is also an enormous push by believers to keep things as they were rather than develop them into what could be. This is why, in the West, efforts to bring Christian churches into line with currently accepted social norms and the wider culturally accepted outlook is proving so difficult. Many members of individual churches are certainly attempting to reshape their beliefs and practices. But once a religion establishes its credo, and uses that credo as a stake that it drives into the cultural ground, it is very difficult for that religion to shift its stake. This inability to shift ground is the reason so many of those brought up religiously no longer attend their church, synagogue or temple. Their church's credo has lost relevance to them as they live their daily lives. As a result, tying their outlook to that particular stake no longer makes sense.

On the other hand, for scientists, challenging assumptions about the world plays a key role in scientific discoveries. Old assumptions are continually examined from new perspectives as new data suggests fresh ways of viewing the world. This leads to new theories. For questioning scientists, even the assumptions of their disciple will eventually be questioned.

On the other hand, many scientists have assumed the scientistic outlook. This limits their investigations to the material sub-domain of reality. For these scientists their assumptions have become a credo, and they have certainly driven that credo as a stake into the ground, to which they have tethered their minds. Such is the limitation they have placed on themselves. But, as noted earlier, in doing so these scientists depart from the scientific method, which is agnostic (that is, is not committed to any assumptions, including the materialist assumptions of scientistic atheism), and so is open to questioning everything, including what is assumed, what is discovered, and what is currently known.

How, then, do assumptions impact on the activity of exploring one's spiritual possibilities?

ASSUMPTIONS IN SPIRITUALITY

As with sciences and religions, spirituality has to make assumptions in order to build a coherent conceptual framework. Spirituality, at least as it is being conceived in these pages, is predicated on the assumption that individuals grow and evolve.

Spirituality is not about finding a handful of concepts that are a good fit with one's current outlook and lifestyle and then using them to justify what one already feels, thinks and does. Rather, spirituality involves questioning one's current lifestyle, attitudes and behaviour, coming to an understanding of what underpins them, and adjusting them so whatever enhances growth is retained and what hinders growth is either corrected or eliminated.

There are many different kinds of practices by which spiritual growth may be facilitated. This is because human beings possess different types of psychological make-up, various forms of cultural conditioning, and as human and spiritual beings have different requirements and needs. The fact is also that different people are at different stages of their spiritual growth and accordingly some individuals need to experience and address one specific set of issues, while others need to experience and address quite different issues.

This is why there have traditionally been so many different religions, and so many sects within each religion. Human psychology, individual life intent, personal requirements for growth, and human and spiritual needs, differ remarkably from one human being to another. One hat, one outlook, one approach, one credo, one stake in the ground, definitely does not suit all.

Nonetheless, in order to progress one needs to make assumptions about what spirituality itself means, what concepts are fundamental to its practice, and what one is required to do in order to grow. For example, the idea that human beings contain a spiritual dimension is an assumption. Clearly, it is not an assumption everyone shares. The just offered suggestion that human beings evolve as spiritual individuals is also an assumption. If the first assumption is not agreed to, then the second assumption becomes meaningless.

This is the way with assumptions. What one person wholeheartedly assumes another dismisses outright. However, neither attitude leads to growth. This is because wholehearted acceptance of what one assumes, and outright dismissal of anything that doesn't accord with one's assumptions, equally keep one in the same place, tied to the same stake one has driven into the ground of one's psycho-spiritual make-up, keeping one thinking, feeling, saying and doing the same things over and over. And inner growth is retarded.

Instead, and this is assuming one wishes to grow, one needs to be open to possibilities that exist outside one's hand-me-down or willingly adopted assumptions. The way to be open is to treat assumptions as propositions.

TREATING ASSUMPTIONS AS PROPOSITIONS

The point repetitiously being made here is that, in order to stimulate one's inner growth, one's assumptions need to be sifted to discover whether they are valid or invalid. Valid assumptions reflect reality and may become the basis for consciously acquiring further knowledge. And invalid assumptions, which diverge from reality, may be adjusted or thrown out.

The process is facilitated by treating one's assumptions not as truths but as propositions. This concept is so fundamental to the outlook offered here that it deserves repeating: To facilitate inner growth you need to transform your key assumptions into propositions. How does this help?

Assumptions are givens. They bolt the armchair of an individual's outlook to a rigidly maintained perspective. As a result everyone observes and interacts with the world from a narrow perspective, through an inflexible framework, ignoring whatever doesn't mesh with that framework. When a human awareness looks at the world "through" a rigid set of assumptions it quite literally does not see much that is before it.

In contrast to assumptions, propositions are not givens. Propositions are provisional statements about the world. Propositions suggest directions to explore. But they don't lock you into anything. They don't bolt you into an outlook from which you cannot shift. Propositions indicate an opening which invites further exploration. Propositions don't present definite answers. Propositions don't close down discussion or enquiry. Propositions leave room for other perspectives. Even for other propositions. Because propositions are provisional and open-ended rather than definitive and closed they are not treated as sacrosanct truths. No one needs to commit their life to them.

If you wish to ascertain whether or not a proposition is valid, you do so by testing it in the appropriate context. Because what is being enquired into here are the fundamental assumptions you make about your life and world, the appropriate place to test them is in the context of your personal life.

For the religious or scientistic who are locked into a credo, such testing is a difficult process, very likely impossible. Why? Because a credo is designed to provide answers. It isn't designed to encourage the questioning of everything, including of the credo itself. But for those who are adventurous, the process advocated here involves transforming beliefs into propositions about the world, then testing those propositions during the course of daily living.

Transforming beliefs into propositions has nothing to do with changing the belief itself. Rather, it requires setting aside attachment to that belief in order to examine it from a variety of perspectives. The aim is to ascertain what that assumption actually involves, including where it came from, how it was formed, what shape it takes within your psychological make-up, and how it impacts on you personally in your life.

This process of enquiry may be likened to the way you examine food you eat. Without inspecting the list of ingredients on the packaging, knowing what country those ingredients came from, what rules governed their growing conditions, and what additives were used when the ingredients were blended, there is no way to know what you are actually eating. In a similar way, investigation is required in order to understand where your beliefs have come from.

The art of examining assumptions is that you need not, indeed must not, have a static relationship with what you believe is true. In the case of anyone pledging themselves to a religious credo of any kind, believers are expected to retain the same fundamental beliefs about themselves and the world throughout their lives. But in the sciences this is not the case. (We are here setting aside the gate-keeping and game-playing individual scientists engage in to compete with, and gain ascendency over, their peers).

The whole point of the scientific method is to continually test one's axioms, to put them at risk of being falsified, in order to gain fuller, more exact, more valid knowledge about the world. As a result of questioning established axioms a scientist may, over the course of a career, end up understanding a particular aspect of reality in quite a different way, and more broadly and deeply, than when he or she began that investigation. Indeed, it could be argued that if, over twenty years of serious investigation, a scientist does not arrive at deeper knowledge, has not adjusted old axioms or proposed new axioms, then he or she has failed at the occupation of being a scientist.

The very same process may be applied to spiritual enquiry. In order to grow as a spiritual identity it is extremely helpful to treat whatever you learn not as a belief or truth into which you may relax feeling that you now know and that's the end of it, but instead maintain the attitude that whatever is discovered is a provisional truth. And when the time comes that provisional truth will itself be examined from various angles, tested to ascertain its ongoing validity, and either adjusted to better fit your new understanding of reality or discarded as outmoded.

In simple terms, this is the basis of the experimental approach to spirituality that is being advanced in this book.

APPROACHING SPIRITUALITY EXPERIMENTALLY

The opportunity exists for anyone to become a spiritual enquirer and, over the course of a lifetime, to go on a journey that begins in a psycho-spiritual state of greater or lesser ignorance and limitation, and that ends, at the body's death, in a state of evolved knowledge and understanding.

It is even possible, indeed it is a commendable aim, that individuals engage so diligently and intently in their chosen field of enquiry or practice that they develop mastery in it. Naturally, this outcome equally applies to all branches of human endeavour, not just the spiritual. And the way to achieve mastery is as a result of testing oneself in the field – the field being the full range of human endeavour.

To summarise what has been stated in this chapter:

- Inner growth as a human being results from enquiring into the bases of your existence and pushing yourself to experience new ways of feeling, thinking and doing. For inner growth to occur, seekers need to appreciate that this is not only possible, it is required.
- Enquiring involves seekers in a process of questioning what they assume, including what they think they know, challenging themselves to enter what they do not know and very likely fear.
- Those tied to a credo don't grow as individuals because they don't challenge their underlying assumptions and so do not open themselves up to new ways of doing, feeling and thinking. Instead, they spend time and effort defending what "they know". Unfortunately, what "they know" has not been arrived at through questioning, but has merely been accepted as being so.
- The scientific method approaches the world experimentally, offering propositions about the world and testing them for validity. This method facilitates the growth of knowledge and of the self that knows, compared to the closed outlook that results from remaining tied to a credo and not challenging one's assumptions.
- The experimental approach to spirituality advocated here asserts that all assumptions, beliefs and axioms should be treated as propositions,

and that these propositions need to be tested and either falsified or shown to be valid. Additionally, the context of validity needs to be clarified, for all valid propositions are valid within certain limitations, which are defined by the question asked and by the activity of testing.

In the following chapters this experimental approach to spirituality will be discussed in much more detail. For now, having completed the discussion about assumptions, we will now present our own first assumption regarding humanity's spiritual nature.

CHAPTER 2

Human Beings
Are Spiritual Beings

THE ASSUMPTIONS UNDERPINNING this view of spirituality begin with the perspective that human identity consists of a spiritual core consciousness existing within an animal body, specifically the body of a species human beings have named homo sapiens sapiens (wise men). While self-selected individuals have certainly achieved levels of mastery that have justifiably led others to call them wise, on the species level this name indicates a potential only. It is certainly not the current prevailing human reality.

Another way of thinking about human beings is to view them as a spiritual core consciousness that enters its host body some time before birth and leaves when that body dies or, in some cases, before the body dies. The physical body is material, the spiritual core consciousness is immaterial. For the duration of a lifetime each human being exists as a coalescence of both immaterial spirit and material body.

It is currently understood that human beings have a physical nature inherited genetically and a psychological nature formed when genetically inherited traits interact with social strictures. To this we add that human beings also have a spiritual nature. Human physical and psychological natures die when the body dies. Spiritual nature does not. Instead, the individual's core consciousness returns to the spiritual domain where it processes what it experienced, spoke, did, felt and thought during its life journey, then prepares itself for incarnation in another body.

This is the fundamental premise for this approach to spirituality. Naturally, in keeping with our experimental approach, we do not ask or expect any reader to accept this premise as a given truth to be swallowed whole. Instead, for now we ask only that readers suspend their natural desire either to believe or to disbelieve and instead maintain an open attitude. Accordingly, ideas as to whether or not God made the human soul, or whether human identity is no more than a chance configuration of genes and social environment, or that consciousness is only an epiphenomenon of the brain and its chemicals, need to be set to one side, at least during the period of digesting this text.

The concept that human beings consist of a physical nature, a psychological nature and a spiritual nature, all intermixed and functioning and manifesting with varying degrees of intensity, gives rise to three related statements about human spiritual nature. These have to do with depth, self-awareness and inner exploration.

DEPTH, SELF-AWARENESS, INNER EXPLORATION

Depth. Human beings contain a depth component that is not always, indeed is very rarely, visible at the physical level of daily living. As a general statement, it may be said that human beings predominantly live on the surface. That is, they live in and through the body and its senses. As a result they struggle to deal with feelings, thoughts and drives that emanate from their own depths.

This is seen in the way that human beings have difficulty perceiving the psychological depths that exist within others, let alone perceiving their own psychological make-up. As for their spiritual depths, it is so foreign to many that they either confuse superficial emotions or ideas with their actual spiritual nature, or they deny possessing a spiritual nature at all. Naturally, denying one's spiritual identity does not affect its ongoing existence.

However, and this is a continuing issue, in general individuals' spiritual core has extreme difficulty making itself heard in the gabble that fills the everyday human awareness. For just as one's body makes its desires known, and one's psychological make-up makes its likes and dislikes and needs known, so the spiritual self communicates its desires, goals and aims into each individual's everyday awareness. But because the spiritual core's communications are very quiet and subtle compared to the body's boisterous sense-centred activities and the constant nattering that occurs within the individual psychological makeup, communications emanating from the spiritual depths are not heard. Or, if they are heard, they are confused with shallower impulses, feelings and thoughts. The reason this occurs is that few human beings are fully self-aware.

Self-awareness. Human beings are normally aware on the sensory level, less aware on the psychological level, and scarcely aware at the level of their spiritual core. So while all human beings possess layers of depth, they are only aware of the shallowest parts of their own deeply layered make-up.

Inner exploration. Spirituality, then, may be thought of as a process of exploring your own depths in order to become more aware of what you are, particularly more aware of the nature of your own self. Spirituality not only puts you in a position to discover more about your spiritual nature, but also to make better use of all the psycho-spiritual resources at your disposal.

In this respect it is important to note that awareness is not identical with consciousness. Consciousness emanates from, and is the fundamental nature of, the spiritual core consciousness. In contrast, awareness (at least, as it is being defined here) is a manifestation of the body's brain and its associated faculties. A brief consideration of what is being termed everyday awareness would be useful at this point. (See FIGURE 2.1)

CONSCIOUSNESS, AWARENESS AND ATTENTION

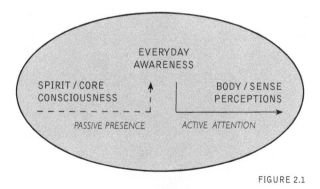

FIGURE 2.1

HUMAN BEINGS LIVE IN EVERYDAY AWARENESS

Everyday awareness is the functioning awareness that people use during the course of their everyday lives. In its most basic sense, everyday awareness is the animal awareness of the individual creature, homo sapiens sapiens.

However, human beings are social animals. Accordingly, enculturation has long been added to the basic human animal awareness. Enculturation includes everything to do with human culture, such as language, dress, traditions, norms of behaviour, and all the complex layers of social interactions that every infant is born into. Enculturation also gives rise to conditioned psychological inputs, including worldview, social and personal attitudes, modes of behaviour and ways of thinking and feeling. In addition, inherited abilities, such as having a family musical or athletic talent, also contribute to an individual's everyday awareness. So the individual human everyday awareness contains layers of bodily and psychological input. Accordingly, human everyday awareness is a complex construct.

Furthermore, each contributing factor is not present simultaneously in the everyday awareness, or always present with the same intensity. This is because only factors that are active during a particular activity, being needed to carry out that activity, contribute to the quality of the everyday awareness at any particular moment.

The result is that during the course of a day the quality of the everyday awareness is constantly changing. For example, waking in the morning and showering and dressing primarily involves motor skills and, perhaps, an aspect of one's socialisation that selects clothes appropriate to the day's activities. During breakfast hunger and taste dominate the everyday awareness, but you may be watching or reading the news as well or planning the day, so the parts of your awareness that are involved in those activities come into play. During the day you might be wholly focused on a complex task, so your everyday awareness is narrowed to using just the aspects required to perform that task. Then, after work, you might go to the gym, or to a movie, or out for dinner, or back home to the family, which activities actively engage the appropriate parts of your everyday awareness.

In this way it can be seen that everyday awareness is not static. While it is grounded in the animal brain's functioning, during the course of any day numerous quite complex social, psychological and feeling, thinking and motor factors become active in your awareness for brief or extended periods, then slip into the background of your awareness as an activity changes and you need to draw on other capacities to carry them out.

Everyday awareness could be likened to a board of coloured lights, in which certain lights turn on in response to a particular situation, then when the situation changes those lights switch off and other lights come on. Except, of course, the lights are layered in depth.

In summary, then, human beings use their everyday awareness to interact with other people, creatures and situations existing in their environment during the course of everyday living.

So where does spiritual consciousness fit into all this?

EVERYDAY AWARENESS AND SPIRITUAL CONSCIOUSNESS

In general, the spiritual core consciousness is not actively present in the everyday awareness during the course of daily living. Rather, it is passively present. That is, it is present, because without its presence the individual would die. But its spiritual level feelings, thoughts and intent are not actively manifest in the everyday awareness.

It is quite possible for the core spiritual consciousness to be present in the everyday awareness. However, for that to occur the everyday awareness would need to be quietened down sufficiently for it to be heard. This usually happens only at times when the individual makes a deliberate effort to quieten all the bodily activities and psychological factors that normally fill the everyday awareness' attention. In the quiet, the whispers of the spiritual consciousness may then become audible.

Hence we observe that, in general, for the vast majority of individuals, the spiritual core consciousness has only a passive presence in relation to the everyday awareness – just like a passive investor who puts money into a business, giving the business its existence and ultimate intent, but doesn't actively participate in its day-to-day running.

We also note that one of the primary goals of exploring one's spiritual nature is to alter this relationship, so that the core consciousness increasingly becomes actively present in, and contributes directly to, daily functioning and decision-making at the level of the everyday awareness. Merging core consciousness and everyday awareness is one of spirituality's ultimate goals.

We'll now consider the next premise, which has to do with the way human beings make sense of the world.

CHAPTER 3

Meaning And Identity
Are Constructed

ONE OF THE BIG ASSUMPTIONS human beings make is that the human brain is capable of arriving at the full truth on the deepest issues, such as the origin and nature of the universe, and how and why reality is as it is. This is an example of a completely erroneous assumption.

The fact is that the human perspective is extremely limited. It has, at best, very limited access to the full extent of what exists throughout reality. This applies equally to religious and scientific "truths". Each offers a perspective and set of explanations, one mythological, the other materially oriented, that can never be more than an angle on reality. Even when knowledgeable individuals achieve a correct view, the human place from which they view reality is on such a slant that their correct view is still a very partial view.

The reason for this is because the human being – and we are referring now to a spiritual core consciousness experiencing physical reality via a human body – can, during the course of everyday life, only perceive using the human body's senses and can only process those perceptions using the human brain.

Human beings quite unquestioningly assume that their human brain is sufficient to arrive at The Truth about reality. Indeed, throughout history pogroms have been initiated because one group violently disagreed with another group's views, so certain were they that they, and only they, possessed The Truth. In fact both sides were always wrong, because the human processing capacity is inherently limited, human perception innately partial, and the human perspective inevitably narrow.

A fallacy exists that both religions and the sciences have long shared. The fallacy is that no other physical life exists in the universe outside this planet. That fallacy has led religions to claim that God has created humanity as a special, privileged and unique race. And they believe that not only has God given dominion to humankind over all other creatures on the Earth, but that all God's hopes for the entire created reality rest wholly in human beings and in none else. This same fallacy of human uniqueness has led scientists, who have not perceived any other life in the universe, to assume that because they can't see it, none exists. Both positions are driven by humanity's self-centeredness backed by limited cognition. And both are completely wrong.

The fact is that the universe is teeming with life and brimming with conscious beings. Cosmologists and astronomers are now beginning to suspect that human beings are not the only self-conscious biological forms in the universe. But it will take some time to process the implication of that fact – which is that however human beings view the universe, it is just one among billions of possible perspectives.

Of course, stating this will not prevent human beings from privileging themselves and their views. After all, and to be fair, the human view is the only view human beings can have. But it might give them pause when they make sweeping generalisations about reality. And it could lead them to hesitate when they claim to know The Truth about anything.

This capacity to exaggerate human significance and perception leads, in extreme cases, to self-delusion. Yet this is actually the flip side of the human desire to make sense of the world in which they live, of the experiences they have, and of their own identity as self-aware beings.

The urge to generate meanings about the world is an inherent aspect of human existence. All human beings constantly recount their experiences, tell stories about what has happened, and seek to make sense of important events. This activity is so embedded in daily life that developmental psychologists call human beings meaning-making animals. This is an apt observation – as far as it goes, because it is yet another limited view.

In fact, it is not the animal part of the human being which strives to make sense of the world. It is actually the spiritual core consciousness residing within the human animal that initiates and drives the human search for meaning. This why the search for meaning is one in which all human beings engage, whether it involves trying to understand simple personal life situations, whether it asks why a friend said or did something, or whether it extends to grandiose efforts to make sense of the world on the cosmic or quantum levels. A consideration of meaning-making will indicate how this is so.

PURPOSE, UNDERSTANDING AND SIGNIFICANCE

For the sake of discussion, meaning-making may conveniently be divided into three principal categories: the search for significance, the search for understanding, and the search for purpose.

The search for significance has haunted human beings from the time they first became the vehicles for spiritual consciousnesses. When a rustle was heard in the undergrowth, when a storm decimated a tribe's camp, when a chance event occurred that helped or hindered them as they sought to fulfil their short-term desires or long-term goals, ancient human beings projected supernatural significance onto these natural events. Clearly, this significance was wholly generated by human hopes and fears.

The search for understanding follows the initial bestowing of significance. Over time individuals realise that the significance they gave to events as children – such as that crashing in the skies is giants fighting, or creaking floorboards under the bed is due to a lurking boogeyman – needs to be replaced by understanding. So the crashing in the clouds comes to be understood as resulting from electrical discharges, and the event that leads to a useful boost in life is understood to result not from the gods' approval but from a complex interplay of factors apparently brought together by intent and chance, each functioning according to its own definable parameters of activity.

Once a degree of understanding is achieved, it is natural for human beings to seek the purpose in what is understood to be occurring around them. Religions and the sciences diverge in their treatment of purpose. Religions happily project purpose onto reality, mostly configuring purpose around, and ascribing ultimate purpose to, their particular concept of God. In the sciences purpose is a difficult notion because the axiom that only matter exists, and that matter is not conscious and so cannot have a purpose, prevents scientists from dealing with purpose at all. So where the religious view the universe as full of God's purpose, the materialist scientist views the universe as purposeless. It could be said that where religions project purpose onto the world, the sciences equally project lack of purpose onto the world. There are slivers of truth in each view, depending on the context and perspective. But there is also much that is fallacious. Here, again, in relation to how purpose functions throughout the universe the human brain flails around, attempting to understand issues that are beyond its ken.

The fact is that the human animal, like all animals, doesn't actually need the activity of meaning-making at all. The human animal doesn't need to generate significance, achieve understanding, or ascribe purpose to what happens around it. Lions, bears, apes, birds, ants and worms don't need significance, understanding or a sense of purpose in order to find shelter, hunt, feed, mate and breed. Neither does the human animal. It is the spiritual consciousness deep within the human body that strives to make sense and generate meaning, using the sophisticated yet inherently limited brain that it has at its disposal to do so.

Accordingly, significance, understanding and purpose are not a given. They do not fall into the human brain like the rain, or automatically grow from a seed of an idea as does a plant. Rather, meaning is a human construct. It is a product of the human brain as it responds to the urge emanating from its buried spiritual core consciousness to comprehend what is happening to it during the course of its existence.

This implies that, in a practical sense, the human capacity to make meaning, while ultimately emanating from the core consciousness, takes place in the everyday awareness. Let's now examine that process.

HOW EVERYDAY AWARENESS CONSTRUCTS MEANING

Meaning does not exist "out there," somewhere in reality, waiting for you to tap into it, in the same way that a fresh water spring waits in the mountains for a tramper to find and drink from. What exists "out there" is the reality that is the universe. Meaning is the sense individuals make of that reality. For human beings, making sense of reality occurs within the everyday awareness.

Each species has its own form of everyday awareness. Flies have fly everyday awareness, dolphins possess a dolphin everyday awareness, dogs a dog everyday awareness, and so on. Each species' everyday awareness is unique. This is due to the combination of: the configuration of each species' sensory perceptual system, the complexity or simplicity of its nervous system, and the power of each species's brain to process its perceptions.

With respect to sensory inputs, flies have spherical eyes to avoid predators and a strong sense of smell to find food. Dogs have very powerful senses of smell and hearing, while eyesight varies between types. Dolphins have very strong hearing, using sonar to guide them while swimming. Humans see colours better than any other animal species, but don't have the detailed sight of an eagle. Due to these differences in sensory input, each species receives quite different perceptions of the world. Different species also possess very different neural wiring and brain capacities for processing and making sense of their perceptions. Yet their life activity is the same, that being to do what all animals do: seek food and shelter, avoid danger, find a mate, reproduce and nurture progeny – or not, if that is their species' behaviour.

The human everyday awareness is associated with a more complex brain and neural wiring than is possessed by any other species on Earth. This enables the human everyday awareness to process quite subtle content out of their perceptions. The result is that sounds are transformed into language, colours are transformed into art, human bodies banging into each other are interpreted as part of a game or as fighting, the way words are spoken is sifted for emotional clues, and squiggles written on paper are interpreted as a poem, a shopping list, a mathematical formula, or a homily.

However, there are also great differences between individuals in the ways they draw meanings from their sense perceptions. A hunter can look into a landscape and see signs of game. A motor mechanic can listen to an engine and diagnose mechanical problems. A musician can look at notation written on paper and produce exquisite sounds. But for others who lack the hunter's experience, the mechanic's know-how or the musician's expertise, the landscape, the motor and the line of notation do not produce the same meanings in their everyday awareness at all. These differences are a function of the differences between individuals' ability to process information in their everyday awareness. And those differences in ability result from the breadth and depth of their experiences and how much they have drawn from their experiences. Basically, these differences reflect how much (or how little) they have learnt and grown.

MEANING MAKING AND GROWTH

Not only do human beings as a species use their everyday awareness to generate meaning out of their experiences of the world, and do so at a more complex level than other Earthly species, but between individuals the capacity of their everyday awareness to perceive and process information varies enormously.

On one level this difference in capacity reflects a natural growth process. The meanings an individual draws from sense experiences during childhood are much less complex than during adulthood. As individuals mature, they undergo a variety of experiences, learn from them, and so deepen their capacity to perceive and draw content out of their experiences. Consequently, their capacity to construct meaning grows. So, to a certain extent, the capacity to process perceptions and construct meaning develops entirely as a natural result of growing from child to adult, from maturing physically and socially. But this type of age related growth is usually limited.

Much more significant is what individuals learn from their life experiences, because learning leads to growth. So the extent to which an individual's capacity to make meaning grows during their life firstly depends on the effort they make to focus their attention on particular aspects of their daily life, and secondly on the extent to which they deliberately work to enhance their capacity to construct meaning. This is clearly the case with the hunter, the mechanic and the musician. During all the years they have trained and worked in their chosen fields of expertise, the hunter, mechanic and musician have enhanced their senses' capacity to perceive specialised information, and they have developed their capacity to process and draw knowledge out of that information.

In fact, this is the purpose of a core consciousness entering a human body: to experience, to focus, to process, to learn, to grow and to gain mastery in chosen fields of endeavour. So while we have asserted that the human perspective is inherently limited in relation to all reality, it is also the case that, within the reality of life on Earth, it is possible to gain mastery of the many situations human incarnation offers, and so to enhance one's human level understanding, while simultaneously reducing one's personal human limitations.

Ultimately, spiritual growth involves gaining mastery over your everyday awareness. Such mastery involves learning to integrate spiritual core consciousness into everyday awareness and its everyday activities. When this occurs your spiritual self contributes to meaning making, so your everyday awareness is no longer filled only with your active human animal and social perceptions and neural processing, your spiritual self also actively contributes to your everyday awareness' deliberations. In this way, the limitations inherent in human perception and cognition may be significantly reduced.

This brings us to consider identity in relation to meaning-making. For just as meanings are constructed, reflecting each individual's distinct capacity to draw meaning out of personal experiences, so human identity is constructed for much the same reasons.

HUMAN IDENTITY IS A CONSTRUCT

In the previous chapter it was asserted that human identity is constructed from assumptions. We now add that to the extent that those assumptions remain unexamined, and to the degree that an individual lives without being aware of them, so the individual's identity remains unexamined and the individual lives unaware of how his or her own identity is constructed.

Human identity is constructed on three levels. The first level is externally constructed. This is physical and social. Physically constructed identity results from the body's basic physiological make-up, which is initially dictated by the genes and is then adjusted by environmental inputs such as quality of food. Socially constructed identity is dictated by the society in which the body lives. Both aspects work together. So what an individual is physically born looking like is altered according to socially dictated parameters. Hence physical looks are altered by clothing styles, by body painting and decorating, by the way head and facial hair is styled, and so on. Socially constructed identity includes many factors, such as status, wealth, sex, schooling, dress, occupation, and so on. All these physical and social factors feed the assumptions people make about their own and others' identity.

The second level consists of self-constructed identity. Some call this self image. It is how you see yourself. Self image is also fed by how you respond to others' perceptions of you. This level of identity is psychological in nature. It includes the obvious traits of possessing confidence or not, of being fearful in certain situations, of hiding inadequacies or, if you have low self-esteem, perhaps drawing attention to your inadequacies to avoid having to do what you are fearful of failing at. A man might be highly competent working with his hands but not so good at thinking, and sees himself accordingly. Or self-deprecation may cause him to underplay his ability with his hands. Or arrogance may push him to view himself as a competent thinker, leading to his self image being at variance with the reality of what he can competently do.

These two levels of identity – the level of external physical and socially projected identity and the level of self-generated psychological identity – are what human beings normally use to construct their individual identity. These two levels are perfectly adequate for dealing with almost everything that human beings experience during the course of their lives, because the huge variety of possible combinations between the two levels affect identity construction massively. That variety accounts for the differences in identity that distinguish one person from another. It also accounts for the frequently wide variation between the identity people give another person and the identity that person gives him or herself. It indicates why what others perceive is sometimes accurate but at other times is wildly off the mark. And it accounts for the way that the identity individuals give themselves, their own self-image, may be accurate or wildly inaccurate.

Complicating the understanding of constructed identity is that it is never static. Identity naturally changes to reflect changes in life circumstances as well as due to aging. How indivduals see themselves, and how they are perceived by others, alters from childhood, through the teen years, into adulthood, middle age and old age. Yet while the levels of physical and social identity are never static, an individual's self identity doesn't usually change to the same degree. The comment has already been made about the differences in an individual's childhood identity and the same individual's adult identity. If individuals don't question or challenge the assumptions inculcated into them during childhood they change little between childhood and adulthood, whereas those who do question their assumptions and examine and challenge themselves may change a great deal.

The effort or lack of effort each person makes to engage with the world and to address limitations in themselves leads to radical or minimal changes in self identity. Those who make a resolute and extended effort generally stand out in some way as greater identities than those who do not do so. In saying this, we do not mean to confuse these "greater identities" with people given high social status or possessing great beauty or wealth. Often "greater identities" remain acknowledged only in the small circle of those who work in the same field of expertise to which they have dedicated themselves. Others may be quite unnoticed. That is all part of the way individual lives play out in the human realm.

However, there is another aspect to all this. This is the third level of human identity construction. It involves the spiritual core consciousness.

Everyday awareness, and the everyday identity associated with that awareness, is wholly focused on the first level of physical and social identity and on the second level of the individual's self image. Accordingly, the contribution core consciousness makes to identity is overlooked.

In fact, the spiritual core has its own identity quite independent of human physical, social and self-generated identity. The spiritual core is an ongoing identity that existed before the individual's body was born and that will continue to exist after that body dies. It might be assumed that, as you become more aware of the spiritual dimension at your core, yet another layer of complexity is added to your identity. Actually, awareness of your spiritual core adds clarity.

This is because as you become more aware of the nature, goals and activities of your spiritual core you gain greater insight into the nature of your life as a human being and into the reasons your identity is constructed the way it is. Much of what appears arbitrary and murky in your life, especially with respect to who you are, who others are to you, the situations you get into, and why you made this choice rather than that choice, begin to be better understood when you start consciously bringing your spiritual identity into your everyday perceptions. Why? Because those people and factors contribute to the life plan you constructed, at the spiritual level, for this particular life journey. This will be discussed at much greater length in the next book in this series, *Practical Spirituality*.

MEANING-MAKING, IDENTITY AND GROWTH

The meanings you draw from your life experiences, along with the identity you construct as a result of learning and growing (as opposed to the identity others project onto you or that you project onto yourself), is a function of what you possess. That is, the meanings you make, and the self you construct, reflect the capacities active within you.

This is the case with those who have a deluded view of the world, such as the schizophrenic and the paranoid. They have a psychological imbalance. Whether that imbalance results from childhood trauma, family or social conditioning, or from chemical imbalances in their nervous or endocrine systems, the result is the same: they project their imbalanced inner state onto the world and behave accordingly, often in a dangerous manner.

This kind of attitudinal projection is actually extremely common. Judging others and finding them guilty in your own mind is an example of psychological projection. So is treating another human being as an animal or less because of their looks, race, lack of wealth or social status. Extreme cases of projection, which lead to obviously unbalanced outlook and behaviour, are easily observed.

However, only slightly less unbalanced perspectives are accepted in a culture if a significant proportion of the population similarly assumes them. This was historically the case with slavery and apartheid. Other examples of socially accepted attitudinal projection include prejudices such as racism, sexism and classism (blaming the poor for their economic limitations is maintained by many of the wealthy). Because the resulting behaviour doesn't break the bounds of acceptable social behaviour scarcely anyone questions such negative projecting. Indeed, politicians and social commentators deliberately tap into imbalanced attitudes, projecting meanings that further reinforce their mutually shared prejudices.

Why are individuals prejudiced, racist, sexist or discriminatory in their outlook, projecting derogatory identity onto others? This behaviour is the result of suppressed and unaddressed psychological traits. Behaviour that puts down another is actually designed to lift oneself up: by lowering another one distracts from and so hides one's own inadequacies. Of course, some inadequacies are real while others are self-projected. But the result is the same: assumed psychological traits result in projected attitudes.

On the other hand, if anyone makes the effort to question their own psychological assumptions, to identify projected attitudes, and then challenge themselves to change unbalanced, negative or self-limiting attitudes, then the underlying psychological assumptions that project those attitudes will vanish. By changing their assumptions and attitudes, they not only eliminate their projections, they change themselves. They then have new internal resources to generate new meanings and identity. And so their overall identity grows.

This same process applies on the wider social level. Unbalanced social attitudes and projections exist because the assumptions that generate them preexist within individuals. The imbalance is generated by a feedback loop: children are raised in communities that teach them to be biased or prejudiced in some way, they absorb those attitudes and are applauded for maintaining them, and they subsequently teach them to the next generation, who they in turn applaud for upholding them. This is how inter-generational ignorance and prejudices are sustained. As was observed earlier, these remain social norms until a small number of individuals initiate a move to reevaluate them. Eventually, the wider community acknowledges the assumed ignorance and prejudice and goes about righting it. In this way communities and nations mature. And group identity grows as a result.

We stated earlier that growth is a natural outcome of experience. So as children grow into teens, then into adults, the meanings they draw from their daily experiences and interactions with others become more subtle and layered. But it is also the case that numerous individuals are walking around in adult bodies, yet the perceptions and the meanings they draw from daily life remain at a childish level.

Some people plainly make more of an effort to comprehend themselves, others and their existence than do others. They pay greater attention to what is happening around them. They are open to what others think, feel and do (in a constructive way, rather than being self-defensive). And they work over what they perceive, grappling with life experiences and thinking them through in order to identity miscommunications and errors in perception and assessment. The deeper meanings they then draw from their perceptions feeds their everyday awareness. As a result they have more to bring to similar future experiences. And so they grow inwardly and are able to achieve more at a greater depth in those activities on which they focus. Eventually, if they keep at it, in their everyday awareness they develop mastery in that particular sphere of activity.

This is what human growth is all about. Inner growth adds to each human being's ability to construct meaning. And because each possesses more within, their individual identity grows. The ultimate aim is to develop mastery at the task of being a spiritual core consciousness residing inside a human body and so to integrate spiritual identity with everyday identity.

The process of growth involves progressively enriching your everyday awareness, which in turn involves making conscious what you previously were not conscious of. As a consequence you enhance your ability to generate meaning. And your sense of your own identity grows, evolving from invalid and fallacious, deluded even, to balanced and perceptive and able to construct meanings that are consistent with the reality of what is occurring around you, within you and beyond you.

An example of how this process occurs is offered by the ways that human beings have thought about God – God long having been considered the source of ultimate meaning and identity.

CHAPTER 4

God Is Not
What You Think

THE ASSUMPTIONS HUMAN BEINGS make about God present one of the greatest hurdles spiritual explorers need to overcome if they wish to achieve a realistic view of reality, understand the nature of their spiritual identity, and appreciate why life events play out the way that they do. For millennia human beings have considered that God, which has been conceived in multiple ways, gives their lives significance and purpose. This is based on assumptions such as that God created them, that God personally guides their life, and that God will reward or punish them according to what they believe and how they act. Of course, many still believe this about God. And many assume that they will be rewarded by God for believing so while those who do not so believe will be punished.

This is childish meaning-making. If any reader assumes the above, this chapter will make for uncomfortable reading.

Historically, humanity has made innumerable assumptions about God. Most of these are projections. For example, all religions propagandise that their religious believers are special to God in a way that other human beings, including believers in other religions, are not. This is apparent when groups refer to themselves as "the chosen people" and when they assert that those who surrender their lives to their God are "saved". This is self-aggrandising posturing that draws on quite specious thinking about God.

If God is considered to be the creator of the universe, human beings can know nothing about God directly. Why? Because the universe is vast, and the creator of that vastness is even vaster. Whereas, as was noted earlier, the human everyday awareness is so limited that it will never be capable of comprehending the scale and detail of what has been created, let alone encompass that which created it. Even the spiritual core consciousness, which is not limited by the human sensory apparatus and neural processing capacity, is unable to comprehend in its fullness the wonder of what is. That wonder is simply too enormous.

In order to deal with this conundrum, historically religions have focused on an individual, such as Jesus Christ, and have conflated that individual with God the creator. Having completed this conceptual sleight-of-hand, Christian believers then worship Jesus Christ as God. In fact, all they have done is reduce the vastness of the creator to human dimensions. This is understandable but deluded. It occurs because the human everyday awareness finds it impossible to envisage anything that is so much greater than itself. Its solution is to reduce the universe, and God the creator of the universe, to its level of comprehension. It reduces the vast unknown to its own minute size. Which means to the dimensions of a human body.

Of course, Christianity is not alone in this. Other historical examples include the Indian god Vishnu, the Greek Dionysius, the Egyptian Horus and the Roman Mithra. Each, like Jesus, was figured as a saviour. And each was conflated with the creator God in an attempt to personalise the impersonal and to domesticate what is beyond domestication. This has occurred throughout history and continues today.

GOD THROUGH THE MILLENNIA

Human beings have always anthropomorphised their environment and projected meanings, specifically human meanings, onto the natural processes occurring around them. The concept of God is no different. A brief survey will indicate the ways the concept of God has changed as human lifestyles and ways of thinking about their world changed.

During the Paleolithic era, when humanity existed in small tribes of hunter-gatherers, they were dependent on animals as a prime source of food. Accordingly, God was thought of as the Lord of the Animals. During the Neolithic era, when humanity began cultivated crops, the cycles of season were anthropomorphised into the triple Goddess of virgin (spring), mother (summer and autumn), and crone (winter). During the Bronze Age, when large cities had formed and kings ruled, God was called the King of Kings and given a role as rewarder and punisher of deeds, just as the kings of city states had power of life and death over their subjects. During this period priests also came to the fore, along with temples to act as the focus of laws. An aristocratic hierarchy backed by priestly bureaucrats organised day-to-day operations, while the soldiery kept the population in line. From this it can be seen that the medieval hierarchies of workers and the ruling and wealthy elites that continue to dominate modern cultures have their roots in Bronze Age city states. In the Iron Age, when populations became educated and started rebelling against the religious and social strictures that controlled them, a number of other gods were added to the distant creator God, with saviour gods such as Jesus and Vishnu becoming significant to the downtrodden.

What this indicates is that, to take the case of Christianity, God the Father, the Ruler of rulers, is envisaged in terms that derive from the Bronze Age, Jesus Christ, the saviour god, comes from the Iron Age, and Mary, the virgin mother, is a conflation of the virgin and mother that dates back to the Neolithic Age. In addition, people today still talk about Mother Nature, another reworking of the Neolithic Goddess concept.

It can be seen that not only did these ideas of God come about as a result of the human everyday awareness making sense of the world using concepts drawn from their then current lifestyles, but once such ideas were formed they remained present in cultural thinking for millennia. These few examples also show the extent to which what people consider to be their personal relationship to God is actually channelled by cultural constructs, which are conditioned into them from birth, and that date back thousands of years.

This is why reviewing one's beliefs, asking where they came from, and grappling with them in order to decide which are valid and useful and which are not, is so important. For no one can journey into new understanding, or see, feel, think or act in new ways, while they are tied to an idea about God that actually is no more than part of an ancient credo, invented by the everyday awareness of their ancient forebears, which today prevents them going anywhere but round and round.

GOD AS IMAGINED DEITY

When considering the notion of God, another key issue is the idea that God is a person. Christian theology refers to God as three persons, while all religions envisage God in human form. Islam is one exception to this general tendency, with believers not being permitted to depict Allah – although in that religion Muhammed and the Qu'ran are revered as sacred in ways that are quite personal, and it is considered that Allah is for believers and against the rest of humanity. So even there biased personal attitudes are projected onto God. The result is that all religions consider that God personally administers to humanity, both on the level of overseeing chosen nations and of individual believers. All this is quite incorrect.

We reiterate: The standard concept of God as a "super person" who cares for individuals personally is a mistaken concept. God the creator is not personal in the way that human beings mean as they generate meaning from the personal perspective of their everyday awareness. This is the activity of the everyday awareness' imagination. It results in imagined deity.

Imagined deity is a projection of human wish-fulfillment. Sigmund Freud was correct when he observed that the personal God of Christianity is a figure conjured up by human beings wanting a perfect, all-loving father to take care of them. (This critique applies to all religions, with the caveat that some add a super-mother to the super-father.) However, Freud was incorrect when he asserted that God is an illusion. This is not the case.

If one considers God to be the creator of all that is, then God certainly does exist. The problem for human beings is that God does not exist in any way that they can understand. Due to the limitations inherent in everyday awareness, God is not what human beings do or can think. And the universe is not created in the ways depicted in religious texts. Or, at least, not in the literal way those religious metaphors are interpreted.

None of this precludes the possibility that human beings are loved and cared for. Human beings, both collectively and individually, are taken care of before, during and after their incarnation in a human body. But the creator is not directly involved in or directly responsible for this caring.

To imagine that the creator is personally involved in a believer's life is akin to a parent thinking that the Minister of Education should be directly involved in their child's education. Or that when citizens have a problem in their lives, the country's Prime Minister or Minister of Finance or Secretary of State will visit their home and solve their problems personally. On the everyday human level this is a ludicrous expectation based in an inflated sense of self worth. Yet believers expect the creator of all that is, in its complete vastness, to pay personal attention to them. This is an example of childish imagination. Yet religions peddle this concept relentlessly.

The reality is that, just as in the human domain the Minister of Health prioritises the country's health budget, and trained professionals are then delegated to administer the actual palliative care, so on the spiritual level trained spiritual beings, existing at a much lower level than that of the creator, respond to human cries for help. Except, of course, where people in the human domain have biases, agendas, blind spots, budget cuts and many other things to distract them or prevent them from fully performing their role, in the spiritual domain this is not the case. Wherever and whenever it is required, spiritual attention, care and love is given to those who need it, without bias, judgement, limitation or expectation of return.

However, even this process can be misunderstood due to imagination. A common error is that because those who are helped have been conditioned by their religion to expect Jesus, or Krishna, or Buddha, or an angel or a saint to answer their call for help, they don't accurately perceive the spiritual identity who has actually comes to their aid. Instead they project their conditioned ideas onto that helping being. Thus they see the Virgin Mary, or Jesus, or Krishna, or Buddha, and so on. This is another by-product of imagined deity.

Of course, many of those who receive assistance don't notice anything at all when a spiritual being helps them. This is largely due to insensitivity resulting from being caught up in the psychological-level nattering that occurs inside their everyday awareness. Equally, it may result from conditioning that tells them such aid is impossible.

In one sense there is nothing wrong with projection. Just as it is okay for children to believe for a time in Santa Claus and the tooth fairy, it is okay for the spiritually immature to believe in some form of imagined deity. It gives them a compass around which to organise their outlook and lives. However, the problem is that children quite easily and naturally grow out of their childhood imaginings about the tooth fairy and Santa Claus. Whereas for conditioned believers to grow out of religiously ingrained imaginings takes great effort, is usually difficult, and often even involves pain.

Why is this? Because those conditioned religious concepts are central to both their everyday meaning making and to their self-image. So deconstructing their conditioned assumptions involves deconstructing their idea of who they are. But everyone is highly invested in their sense of their own identity. This is why dismantling and rearranging beliefs is such a difficult and painful task. Coming to a valid and correct view of reality, and of the creator of reality, ultimately involves challenging one's most intimate sense of self.

GOD IN REALITY

The nature of God is not easily explained. To say that God is the creator of all that is, as we have blithely been doing, is not actually a coherent statement. It begs further questions, such as: What precisely is the nature of all that is? What is the process of creation? How does God initiate and manipulate that process? And what is the nature of God that God is able to do so? We have attempted to answer these questions, at least in part, in the books *The Matapaua Conversations* and *The Kosmic Web*. However, even these attempts have had to speak to, and make allowances for, the limited nature of human everyday awareness.

The human awareness has more concepts at its disposal today than were available even one hundred years ago, and in the future it will have even more concepts useful to subsequent attempts to understand the nature of all that is. So while we direct those who are curious about the nature of God to *The Matapaua Conversations* and *The Kosmic Web*, we also acknowledge that those texts put forward no more than a series of provisional statements that will be superseded at a later date.

Nonetheless, for individuals grappling with their own conditioned concepts about God and reality, what is offered in those two books is still likely to be far in advance of their current understanding. This is as it should be, because it is only when a majority of spiritual explorers catch up with a new conceptual framework such as is offered in *The Matapaua Conversations* and *The Kosmic Web*, and when the human everyday awareness has newer ruling concepts that require such a framework's updating, that an even newer configuration of anciently understood truths will be constructed to aid embodied individuals in their efforts to comprehend who, what and why they are, what reality is, and what is the relationship of the creator to all that is.

In the meantime, those texts are entirely capable of challenging any enquirer's current assumptions about the nature and activity of God.

FOUR IMPLICATIONS

CHAPTER 5

Maturing Is A Journey From Belief To Knowledge

B Y NOW IT WILL BE PLAIN to readers the extent to which beliefs of all kinds are naturally generated by the human everyday awareness during its daily interactions. Many beliefs are totally innocuous, such as the belief that an apple a day will keep the doctor away. Other beliefs involve practical necessities, such as the belief a light will turn on when you flick the switch. And some beliefs reflect truths about the world, such as the belief that the Earth travels around the Sun. In this last case such belief is better described as knowledge.

As was stated earlier, a particular belief is no more than an assumption until it has been tested and the tester has ascertained whether or not it reflects reality. Tested and validated beliefs become the basis of new knowledge. Because individuals have different experiences, and because people often draw quite different conclusions from the same experiences, there is an extensive range of positions from belief to knowledge. And even within this range there are those at the extremities, such as those who espouse lunatic beliefs and those who express extensively tested knowledge. This latter category applies both to knowledge obtained through objective scientific testing and to knowledge garnered as a result of interrogating one's own assumptions and outlook and tempering them in the fires of personal experience.

It is, of course, mere common sense to draw attention to this range from the lunatic to the knowing. Anyone who gives the idea a moment of attention can easily verify it from their own experience, and can further verify how the very different functioning of people's everyday awareness accounts for the huge differences between assumed beliefs and hard won knowledge. Accordingly, from the spiritual perspective advocated here, the principal point that needs to be made is that beliefs are held by immature individuals or cultures. whereas knowledge, particularly knowledge that is hard won, is in the possession of the mature.

When two people argue over their belief or non-belief in God they are each indulging in childish behaviour – because they are arguing over beliefs, not knowledge. Of course, each side maintains what they believe with great intensity. Each considers they know The Truth and that those they oppose do not. But thinking you know is not the same as actually knowing. Neither is holding intensely to a belief the same as actually knowing.

Until a belief has been rigorously tested it is nothing more than an assumption. And an assumption should be considered as only a starting point on the journey towards knowledge. This is the journey from immaturity to maturity. The discoveries of Copernicus provide an example of this journey.

FROM BELIEF TO KNOWLEDGE

When Copernicus first proposed that the then current geocentric view was wrong (that the Sun, Moon, planets and stars all circled the Earth) , he had no empirical verification that his new proposal was correct. Indeed, he began investigating the idea that the Earth circles the Sun because he read it in Pythagorean literature. So he started with a belief. He then developed this belief into a model, intellectually working out how it would work if it was correct. But it wasn't until Galileo built a telescope and observed moons circling Jupiter, Mercury traversing the Sun, and observed the phases of the planets, that empirical confirmation for Copernicus' proposition was obtained.

Interestingly, however, there was a fundamental limitation in the thinking of Copernicus and those who followed him. This was they assumed that the planets would orbit the Sun in perfect circles. This assumption came from Christian theology, which itself was derived from the ancient Greeks. They all assumed that because God the creator was perfect, anything God made would also be perfect. Further assuming that the circle was the most perfect form, they concluded that the planets would naturally orbit the Sun in circles. It was only after Kepler realised that planets travel in ellipses that this assumption was shown to be false and that correct knowledge of the planets' orbital paths was arrived at.

Newton later perfected the mathematical description that Kepler developed. Newton's mathematical laws remained the accepted truth for one hundred years, when new measurements of Mercury's orbit showed anomalies that indicated Newton's mathematical modelling was not fully correct. It was only when Einstein proposed his theory of relativity that the reason for the anomaly was understood and a new accepted truth was achieved.

It can be seen from this example that there was a considerable journey from belief to knowledge. At each stage it was only by thinking, modelling, observing, questioning, proposing new concepts, and testing those concepts, that a progressively more precise explanation was arrived at. At each stage achieved knowledge proved not to be The Truth, but to be a provisional truth, which itself needed to be adjusted as further information was obtained and more exact knowledge was achieved.

Historically, humanity's journey from belief to knowledge has been fraught with mistakes, power plays, grandstanding and sheer bloody-mindedness – on the part of those who relentlessly sifted their beliefs in search of ever more accurate knowledge, and on the part of those who would stop them from discovering it. Nonetheless, it is a journey that has to be made, on both the collective and individual levels, in order to grow from child to adult.

A society matures when its traditions, norms and laws, along with its descriptions and explanations of reality, increasingly derive from knowledge rather than from belief. And an individual matures when conditioned assumptions adopted as beliefs are replaced by knowledge gained through experience.

It is never easy bucking beliefs when others around you not only assume certain things to be true, but when they subtly or boorishly coerce you to conform to what they believe. And it is even more difficult to buck personal conditioning and the assumptions that underpin personal identity. This is why knowledge is always hard won.

BELIEFS AND FEAR

Why, then, do beliefs exist? What is their purpose? Are they spiritual? The fact is, beliefs have no spiritual purpose. They are entirely a by-product of the limitations inherent in the human everyday awareness. And the dominant driver of that awareness is fear. We will examine fear and the way it distends the human psychology in detail in *Practical Spirituality* and *Psychological Spirituality*. But it is pertinent to make a few preliminary points about fear here because it is certainly relevant to this discussion.

Human fear derives ultimately from the brain stem, which is also known as the old or reptilian brain. This is where the basic fight or flight emotions reside. These originally helped all animals, not just the human animal, survive when their life was threatened. The brain stem responds to physical threats by pumping adrenaline into the body. As a result the senses and reactions become much sharper than normal and the animal becomes more effectively able to defend itself, whether by fighting or by running away.

But as human beings multiplied, and safety in numbers reduced the physical threats in their environment, the basic animal fear wasn't needed as often. Instead, that animal fear became socialised. Thus the ancient tribal impulse of defending one's home and feeding territory was socialised into the combat that is sport, in which one's club and sporting reputation is defended. However, while physical threats to human life is rare in civilised nations today, as anyone can readily attest fear continues to readily well up whenever human identity feels threatened.

In a much wider existential sense it could be said that human beings suffer the fear of being alone and abandoned in the world. Feelings of rejection frequently negatively impact on an entire life, leading to ruinous outcomes. This same feeling of rejection also occurs on a spiritual level. When a spirit is embodied for the first few times it is extremely uncertain of itself and as a result finds it difficult to cope with coarse bodily sense-based experiences – coarse, that is, compared to its prior experiences as a non-embodied spirit. Such spirits do not know how to control their body and have to undergo the difficult process of learning how to use their body to interact with others. Only gradually, over successive incarnations, does a spiritual identity begin to learn how to function as a spiritual core consciousness within a human body perceiving via the constricted conditioned human everyday awareness.

What makes this situation even more fraught is that to its own initial uncertainty and fear of being in a body is added the animal fear responses emanating from the brain stem. For a long time these two sources of fear, one animal, the other resulting from the experience of being embodied, can reinforce one another and lead to excessive defensive behaviours, including a ready use of violence to defend against perceived threats, whether those threats be real or imagined.

Over a series of lives, as familiarity with the state of embodiment grows, and especially as the individual learns to better control the body in which it dwells, and its biological and psychological impulses, the initial ready resort to physical violence diminishes and fears are socialised into behaviours that are socially acceptable. Thus changes in a social environment, in which conflict ceases to be resolved by violence and instead is resolved in socially constructive ways, actually occur as a result of the majority of individuals in that community or nation maturing. Another example of this maturing process is that today a worker is an employee who is fired if he doesn't perform, whereas in earlier times such a person was a slave whose poor performance resulted in him being beaten to within an inch of his life. Or worse. While the most violent expressions of fear are an exception rather than the rule, the fact remains that fear continues to bubble under all experiences, ready to jump to the forefront of everyday awareness whenever threats occur.

The natural way of dealing with fear is to cover it up. This is what defensive behaviour is: an attempt to bury the fear that otherwise too readily wells up into everyday awareness. But the problem with covering up fear is that it doesn't actually remove the fear. All it does is transform felt fear into suppressed fear. And that suppressed fear continues to percolate within. It then subtly or not-so-subtly infiltrates an individual's psychological makeup, influencing feelings, thoughts and decision-making.

How does this fear relate to beliefs? Beliefs can be seen as a form of psychological self-calming. Inventing and clinging to beliefs is a socialised way of dealing with threats so that individuals are not overwhelmed when existing in a frail body itself constantly threatened by an unknown, powerful and consequently scary world. Ultimately, beliefs are invented as a way of coping with the fear of being human.

In ancient times, when a storm decimated the tribal camp, the storm was given a personal identity and name, such as a god like Indra or Thor. Sacrifices were offered to appease that imagined god with the hope that the camp would not be threatened by storms again. Today, when people fear losing control over their life, or fear not getting what they want, or when they fear others they love won't achieve what they want, they equally pray and offer sacrifice to an imagined deity. Sacrifice may involve making obeisance, making offerings, fasting, or surrendering part of their life in ritual service.

Thus belief in a personal God was always, and continues to be, an attempt to cope with the fear of the unknown. This fear involves feelings of helplessness that are generated when individuals don't understand why horrible things happen to them and those they love. Believing they are protected by their God, and therefore that the worst won't happen, helps human beings suppress their fear and cope with the troubles of daily life. If they weren't able to suppress their fear via their beliefs, that is, if their fear of the uncontrolled unknown was always present in their everyday awareness, they would go mad.

In this sense, belief is a mat that believers pull over the hole at the centre of their everyday awareness, a hole in which unspoken, often unspeakable, fears lurk. This is why believers hold so fast to their beliefs. No matter how rationally they may be able to justify their beliefs to others, inwardly they have a hole at the centre of their identity, a hole they have to hide.

The problem is that pulling up the rug of their beliefs to hide their fears will never make those fears go away. What everyone actually needs to do is to pull the rug away, shrug off their everyday self's attempts at self-calming, and confront what they fear. Why? Because this is how human beings mature: by eradicating fear through knowledge.

USING KNOWLEDGE TO VANQUISH FEAR

The way to vanquish fear is through dissolving it in knowledge. For example, if a child is scared of the boogeyman hiding under the bed a parent can shine a torch under the bed to show that nothing is there. Perhaps the parent may even leave a light on at night until that knowledge is reinforced through repetition and the child can see that the fear, which is a fear of being attacked that ultimately emanates from the brain stem, is purely imaginary.

Just like that child who has to be shown nothing is under the bed, so enquiring individuals need to pull back the rug of beliefs that cover their fundamental fear, address the self-defensive behaviours that prevent them from doing so, shrug off their everyday self's continued attempts at self-calming, and confront what they most fear. By doing so they will eventually overcome their fears. Just like the imagined boogeyman who the torchlight causes to fade away, so the sustained light of self-investigation will eventually dissolve the fears that rake them.

Of course, fear is so deeply ingrained in the immature human psychology that there is considerable fear of confronting the fear. There is an old saying, "Better the devil you know than the devil you don't know". This is merely another manifestation of the fear of the unknown, seemingly rationalised into common sense. It actually represents an attempt to self-calm – because both the devil you know and the devil you don't know are manifestations of the same deep fear of being in a strange, dangerous and uncontrollable world.

Hence when people say "Better the devil you know than the devil you don't know", what they are actually admitting is that they are too scared to give up the fear they know because that fear, however horrible it may be, gives them an anchor in the world. They don't like the fear, but they have developed strategies to cope with it. They have made it familiar. They have domesticated it. Of course, the fear may very occasionally well up and overcome them, but as long as they don't challenge themselves, as long as they stay in the safe bounds of the known, they can largely keep it and their lives under control. Whereas if they gave up their "domesticated devil" where would that leave them? To use another vernacular favourite, they would be "up the creek without a paddle".

This is why so many people can't bear the idea of giving up their fear-generated beliefs. They feel they need their fear-generated beliefs to help them paddle through life. Even when that paddle is purely imagined. Without the paddle all they have is the unknown. And that scares them silly.

Testing one's erroneous beliefs and abandoning those that are biased, limiting, injurious or outright vile is a complex task. But once it is achieved it is like stepping out of shadow into sunshine. Individuals then open themselves up to ideas, feelings and experiences they could never previously have conceived. Their blinkers having been discarded, and having walked away from the constricting armchair in which they sat for so long, they will realise that there is so much more to perceive, experience, wonder at and enjoy than they previously ever envisioned. Indeed, they will wonder what took them so long to abandon their self-limiting beliefs, so long to escape being in thrall to their fear.

Knowledge has this impact. Not because it provides final truths – we have already noted the provisional nature of all knowledge and every truth – but because knowledge opens up new vistas to experience and new opportunities to feel, think and act. This in turn leads one towards even more distant vistas and ever more fascinating experiences.

The individual who lives at the bottom of a valley, in perpetual shade and fog, tied to the stake of what they believe, remains there because it is what they are familiar with and because they are fearful of abandoning it and entering the unknown. Yet if they were able to leave the safety of their narrow existence, halfway up the mountain they would clear the clouds and find another larger village, wonderful teeming meadows, and yet more villages and valleys stretching beyond what the eye can see.

It is a vicious feedback loop: individuals cling to the certainties of their beliefs to suppress their fear, but that fear keeps them from addressing the beliefs they need to question in order to escape their fear. And while knowledge will shine a light on beliefs, dissolving both them and the fear that underpins them, fear cowers everyone and stops them from turning on the light in the first place.

In the next chapter we will examine how to side-step fear in order to question beliefs and achieve knowledge.

CHAPTER 6

The Human Self Is Layered

O NE OF THE BIGGEST FEARS human beings have is the fear of entering their own self. Everyone knows it's dark in there. You close your eyes, sense-bearings vanish, and what becomes present is blackness, like in a cave, in which who knows what unknown dangers lurk, waiting to jump out and shock you!

Entering the self may be likened to the Greek myth of the labyrinth. According to the myth, Daedalus originally built the labyrinth as an intricate maze so the monstrous Minotaur trapped at its centre could not escape. Sacrifices were made to the Minotaur to appease its hunger and so prevent it seeking to escape to find food.

This myth is replicated in the human psychology. Each individual human being has a suppressed fear lurking at the centre of their psychology, around which is arrayed an intricate pattern of defensive behaviours. Holding fast to beliefs is one among the many defensive behaviours that are maintained to keep the underlying fear suppressed and the Minotaur at bay. All individuals spend a significant portion of their daily life sacrificing time and energy in order to appease the Minotaur of hidden fear, defending it and keeping it concealed not just from civilised society, but also from themselves.

In the myth Theseus eventually killed the Minotaur. But he was able to do so only because Ariadne gave him a thread which he rolled out as he entered the labyrinth so he could find his way back out after he had killed the Minotaur. Without the thread he would have been lost forever in the labyrinth.

The thread is the key here. With the thread the adventurous Theseus knew how to return to safety. In order to enter and explore the labyrinth of the self, eventually finding and killing the fear that lurks at its heart, then be able to travel back, one needs the psychological equivalent of a thread. This is supplied by a practical model of the self. With a model you remain oriented as you journey within, and you have a clear way of returning to your starting point. Even when you enter previously unknown caves within your self, a practical model will provide a clear frame of reference to show you where you are. In this way a model becomes a kind of map, which helps combat the fear of entering the unknown that is the self.

In this chapter we offer such a guiding model of the self. The purpose of the model is to function as a generalised map so spiritual explorers may enter within and not feel afraid. Because, of course, feeling you might get lost brings up fear which causes you to hesitate.

What is the model? We observed earlier that human identity has three layers, consisting of bodily identity, socialised psychological identity and spiritual identity. However, even this is not sufficient to capture the full complexity of psycho-spiritual processes that occur within the full human identity. Therefore we now present a model that draws out the implications of the ideas offered in the previous chapters.

INTRODUCTION TO THE FIVE-LAYERED SELF

In this model the self consists of five layers: the biological self, the socialized self, the essence self, the energetic self and the spiritual self.

The *biological self*, more commonly known as the body, is grounded in the human animal, homo sapiens sapiens. The human brain contains three layers: the old brain, also known as the reptilian brain; the limbic system, also known as the paleo-mammalian brain; and the neo-mammalian brain, more commonly known as the neo-cortex. These three parts of the human brain act together to facilitate the receiving, processing and passing on of complex information.

The nature of the biological self is fundamentally dictated by genetically inherited traits. However, influences external to the DNA affect the expression of genes during the body's growth. For example, famine will alter the body's inherited features. Deprived of vital minerals and trace elements, the body's growth is stunted. Equally, emotional trauma will disrupt important emotional connections in the limbic system and prevent its normal development. If the trauma is sexual in nature, then aversion or even fear may come to the fore during adult sexual relationships and disrupt normal sexual responses.

The *socialized self* is a psychological and behavioural layer that is shaped by the social conditions into which the body is born and develops. This self is conditioned by and reflects the local physical and social environments. Language, education, family, social norms, work, opportunities, and so on all contribute to the formation of the socialised self. So where the biological self is shaped genetically, the socialised self is shaped by social and environmental conditioning and by the way the individual responds to that conditioning. The self-image noted earlier is a function of the socialised self.

The *essence self* consists of the higher human capacities of the biological self. This layer of the self is where human beings grow practically, emotionally and intellectually. It is the essence self that is educated and that learns, develops abilities and matures as an individual.

The biological self is largely mature by the age of eighteen. In contrast, the socialised self is labeled as adult at the symbolic age of twenty-one. In fact it never matures. This is because it is formed as a negotiation between the essence self and the social environment. And it only ever changes as much or as little as is required to maintain its ongoing identity. Two examples indicate the extremes of no change and radical change.

When individuals migrate from one country to another many attempt to preserve their culture, retain friends and source food from their home country, and even speak their own language as much as possible. Such migrants don't want to give up their culture because they feel it is their identity. This is preserving everyday identity as it is centred on the socialised self.

At the other end of the scale is the situation of soldiers going to war. In theatres of war soldiers find that the everyday social environment they have long been accustomed to has changed suddenly and radically. Some then lose their moral compass and engage in actions they would not carry out under normal circumstances. For these individuals their sense of identity, as with migrants, is centred on their socialised self. But the social conditions generated by being at war ruptures their sense of themselves as a social identity. Old brain blood lust may also overpower their normal socialised behavioural norms. Ungrounded, their behaviour may change to such a degree that they don't even recognise themselves. The socialised self can slide from confident to bereft, from easy-going to vicious, in an astonishingly short time.

In contrast, this type of disruption or clinging to patterned social behaviour is not such an issue for the essence self. Unlike the socialised self, it isn't wholly conditioned and doesn't automatically seek to cling to what it is. As the essence self undergoes experiences and learns from them, it matures and grows and gains a correspondingly stronger sense of what it is. If the essence self grows sufficiently to dominate the everyday awareness, that individual's awareness is well grounded and able to cope with changes in the environment, such as migrating to a new country or going to war, and retain its sense of self identity. However, in most people it is the biological and socialised

MODEL: THE FIVE LEVELS OF THE LAYERED SELF

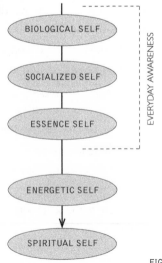

FIGURE 6.1

selves that dominate the everyday awareness, with only slivers of the essence self making an impact. [See FIGURE 6.1]

The *energetic self* stands between the three layers of the biological, socialized and essence selves on one side and the spiritual self on the other. That triad of layers is sufficient for an individual to live a perfectly accomplished and satisfactory life. Those three layers in themselves deliver rich experiences and provide much material for an individual to work on. But for those who wish to appreciate their spiritual nature, an understanding of the energetic self is crucial.

The energetic self is more commonly known as the aura. It conveys information between the spiritual domain occupied by the spiritual self and the physical domain occupied by the biological, socialised and essence selves. The energetic self makes possible many things. Because we have already commented on the aura's nature and purpose in *The Matapaua Conversations* and *The Kosmic Web*, we will not repeat them here. Suffice to say that it is a conduit between the spiritual and physical domains.

The *spiritual self* is the core consciousness. It is a fragment of a more extensive spiritual self that takes on a series of bodies for the opportunities human incarnation provide to experience, learn and evolve. The spiritual self chooses the body, the social conditions, and the essence qualities it wishes to use in any particular life. Lives are planned in broad strokes and in fine detail. However, much can go awry. Opportunities are missed and plans may not be realised. This is especially the case when the spiritual self is unable to manifest in an individual's everyday awareness and so is unable to contribute to the choices the individual makes.

We will deal extensively with the influence of the spiritual self on an individual's life journey in the next book in this series. For now we wish make a few more comments on the nature and functions of the socialised, essence and spiritual selves.

THE SOCIALIZED SELF

For the majority of human beings their sense of identity primarily consists of their body and their socialised self. Human beings are social animals and everything is expressed via their social self. Culture, language, norms, work and conditioned behaviour are all key to the shaping and functioning of the socialised self.

Biological sexual urges are socialised during the teenage years, followed by developing relationships, getting married and raising children. The urge to reproduce and nurture children is socialised into sustaining a legally approved relationship, renting or buying a house, working to support children and spouse, and innumerable other related activities.

Essence talents are similarly expressed via the socialised self. So a child may have a natural talent for art or gardening. That talent is then nurtured through schooling and peer interactions, or suppressed because the social environment is not conducive to the development and expression of that particular talent. It may be that the child's parents can't afford art lessons, or the child might have to work and forego schooling, or a traumatic incident may occur that shatters the child's self-confidence and as a result the child suppresses his or her own essence drive.

BIOLOGICAL SELF	SOCIALIZED SELF
BIOLOGICAL GIVENS	**SOCIAL GIVENS**
Brain and central nervous system	Tribe/nation
Endocrine system	Technological environment
Genetically determined qualities	Social norms
Effective condition and functioning of body	
	SOCIALIZATION PROCESSES
BIOLOGICAL DRIVES	Education
Food and water	Family, peer and cultural conditioning
Territory	Status
Personal/family shelter	Repression and transformation of biological
Reproduction and nurturing of offspring	drives into socially accepted behaviours
Dominance to protect offspring	Developing ethical values, including tolerance
Adaptation to environment	and hatred
BIOLOGICAL INSTINCTS	**RESPONSES TO SOCIALIZATION**
Sex	Socialized personal goals
Territorial acquisition and defence	Personal adjustments to conditioning
Bodily survival, including fear and the urges	Sexual identity/orientation
of flight and/or flight	Formation of defence mechanisms
Display	Formation of attitudes, including prejudices
	and fixed attitudes towards self and others

FIGURE 6.2

This is the sense in which the socialised self is a negotiation between the essence self and the social environment. The socialised self channels essence urges and desires, either promoting or inhibiting their expression. Inhibition is largely influenced by fears, whether they be fears others project onto the individual or that the individual fans within him or herself. The stimulation of essence urges depends on there being a nurturing social environment. Or, at least, not a de-powering and inhibiting social environment.

There is no set formula for what conditions are actually best for an individual to grow. Some individuals chose an inhibiting or non-nurturing environment in order to have significant obstacles to overcome. This keeps them focused on their main task and forces them to keep up their efforts. Others choose a supportive social environment because that is what they best need to develop their abilities. The choices are made by the spiritual self when it weighs up its goals prior to incarnating. In practice, most people choose a life in which there is a mix of inhibiting and nurturing factors, sufficient to focus their attention but not too much to discourage them altogether, nor too little that it all becomes so easy that they fall into laziness.

Even this expression of spirituality, this book, has been manifested within the bounds of the socialised self. The language and concepts used, the fact that we are free to discuss such matters in this way without being censored, are only possible because our scribe lives in a conducive social environment.

In this sense, it can be understood that a spiritual communication such as this can only be conveyed between human awarenesses using the socialised self. However, such spiritual level communication requires that the socialised self remain passive. If, for example, the socialised self of our scribe interfered, by changing comments to appeal to more people, or to enhance its own self-image, or because he feared generating offense, then the effectiveness of this communication would be reduced.

Accordingly, the art of spiritual exploration involves establishing a balance between the five layers of the self so the spiritual self may live this life to its optimal potential. This issue of interference between layers will be explored in the following chapter. For now we'll further discuss the essence self.

THE ESSENCE SELF

There are many ways of dividing the range of human capacities. Utility and aptness to the prevailing cultural outlook are the two principal factors that decide in favour of one way over another. We assert that the essence self may be divided into three capacities, which provide three separate means for processing experiences and expressing intent. These three capacities are moving, emotional and intellectual. That human beings naturally possess these three capacities is easily understood. And these three are also consonant with a developmental model of the self, which is instrumental to our approach here.

The moving capacity is used in all the practical activities of daily life: dressing, working, preparing meals, cleaning up. Occupations that utilise the moving capacity include carpentry, cooking, mechanical engineering and sport. There are also higher level moving skills, such as a builder uses to translate a two-dimensional plan into a three-dimensional building, or when an artisan manipulates materials to produce specialized or artistic objects. When constructing time-frames and budgets, abstract moving thought is used. So a range of levels are involved in the moving capacity, from the entirely physical, to manipulating materials for emotional effect, to the conceptual.

The emotional capacity is basic to socialisation. Human beings communicate emotionally most of their waking existence. They even continue emoting in their dreams, when suppressed anxieties and fears may come to the fore. Some individuals have a predilection for the emotions, working as teachers, social workers, performers, communicators and nurturers of all kinds. The emotions also involve higher levels of functioning, such as the empathetic appreciation of others' emotional states. Artistic expression may or may not involve higher level emotional functioning.

The human intellectual capacity manifests in a wide range of conceptual pursuits and occupations, such as mathematics, philosophy, theology and physics. It needs to be noted that an intellectual aspect is also present in the moving and emotional capacities. In moving activities intellect manifests as planning and common sense appraisals, while in emotional activities it manifests as intuition. Where planning is pragmatic and intuition functions in flashes, pure intellectual thought is comparatively more methodical. Accordingly, it takes longer to work through an issue. But it offers the ability to bring together a wider range of elements than pragmatic planning and intuition are capable of. This framework we are offering here is principally expressed via the intellect. But to this expression are added intuitive insights and an occasional splash of plain common sense.

One of the keys to appreciating the way the essence self functions is that the moving, emotional and intellectual functions overlap. This can result in low level dysfunction, when individuals attempt to use their emotions rather than their moving capacity as they attempt to solve a practical problem, or when they try to reason their way through an emotional situation. It leads to high level functioning when the three capacities are drawn on appropriately, with one becoming active to deal with a situation, and the others becoming passive. Then, when a new situation is faced, another more appropriate capacity comes to the fore and the others recede into the background.

Low level functioning occurs because people naturally have a preference for one capacity over the other two. The result is lopsided functioning, such as when a builder is very accomplished with his hands, and astute in managing practical schedules, but hopeless when discussing the politics of the day because he isn't capable of using his intellect to work through concepts, and at home he is unable to use his emotions to communicate with his children. Few people are equally developed and balanced in all three capacities.

This is why a developmental model applies to the essence self. As individuals undergo a variety of experiences, process those experiences, learn from them, and work to do better next time, they feed their essence self. As a result of this feeding, their moving, emotional and intellectual capacities grow. Fundamental to this growth is overcoming negativities in the forms of addictions, prejudices, biases, self-defensiveness, fantasising and so on. We will look at these in a little more detail in the next chapter.

For now it is sufficient to conclude by reiterating that the essence self is where an individual grows as a human being. And as more of the essence self actively manifests into the everyday awareness, so that awareness deepens and increases its awareness ever more extensively and subtly.

THE SPIRITUAL SELF

To complete this very brief introduction to the model of the five layered self, we will comment a little more on the spiritual self. The purpose of engaging in spirituality is not just to talk about spiritual matters, nor to study spiritual literature, nor to follow other people who are generally agreed to be spiritual. The purpose of engaging with spirituality is to contact your own spirit. This series of books has been designed to show how this may be done.

The spiritual self has experienced far more than has any individual's everyday awareness. Consequently it knows much more than the information that is available to the human everyday awareness. Part of the task of spirituality is to bring into active awareness knowledge of the fact that each and every human being possesses, indeed is, a spirit. Prayer is one way of doing this, although the strictures of religion and the desires of the socialised self tend to interfere so much during the activity of prayer that the subtle voice of the spiritual self is prevented from being heard. Meditation is more effective,

ESSENCE SELF	SPIRITUAL SELF
ESSENCE GIVENS Moving capacity Emotional capacity Intellectual capacity (Each potentially at independent levels of development: infant, child, teenager, adult)	**SPIRITUAL GIVENS** Spiritual level consciousness Is intrinsically loving Has experienced multiple incarnations Uses incarnation to evolve

INNATE ESSENCE ABILITIES
Predilection towards moving, emotional or
   intellectual capacities
Physical, emotional, or intellectual talents
Inner balance between three capacities
	LIFE INTENT
	Pre-selects body, social environment, essence
	   qualities
	Uses body, socialised self and esence self to
	   form a new sub-identity
	Sets specific goals to achieve in each life
	Attempts to link with the essence self in order
	   to achieve those goals

ESSENCE GOALS
To develop innate essence talents, abilities
   and capacities
Fulfil personal life goals
Transformation and sublimation of biological
   drives and social construction of self
	LIFE PROCESS
	Faciliates its own evolution by infusing every-
	   day awareness with its intent
	Prompts the sub-identity to transcend its bio-
	   logically and socially constructed layers
	Uses limiting factors to enhance its growth

FIGURE 6.3

because it involves shutting down inner chatter and creating an open space for the spiritual self to speak.

The early stages of spiritual exploration involve opening up everyday awareness to input from the spiritual self. The various non-ordinary perceptions people initially have of love, or of greater levels of consciousness, perhaps even of ecstasy, are all experiences generated by their own spiritual self.

There is much confusion over this because people frequently project such perceptions onto their spiritual teacher, onto deceased saints, or even onto God. The fact is that compared to the limited everyday awareness, based as it is in the human brain and nervous system, the spiritual self possesses a far greater degree of consciousness and perception, is intrinsically loving, and is aware of much more, than the human everyday awareness is ordinarily capable of processing.

This is why we assert that the aim of spirituality is to infuse the everyday awareness with ever more input from the spiritual self. But for this to occur, seeking individuals need to stop holding so tightly to their biological and socialised selves. Only by letting go can deeper levels of the layered self become activated and begin to manifest in the everyday awareness.

What prevents letting go? Fear is again the prime culprit here. The degree to which fear infiltrates the everyday awareness is indicated when we consider individuals' attitudes towards dying. So many people are fearful of dying. And they fear dying because they fear losing their identity as a body and as a social being who has relationships with other people, bodies, places and things.

In fact, an individual's identity in this life is just one sub-identity in a series of sub-identities that each and every spiritual identity experiences. So while many assume that their sub-identity in this life is their only identity, and so cling to it for dear life, it is actually no more, and no less, than one sub-identity in an ongoing series of sub-identities.

Fear clouds this fact, whether by manifesting as the denial that individuals continue to consciously exist once the body dies, or else by inventing all kinds of fantasies about what happens to individuals after their body and its associated sub-identity is no more. There is nothing to fear. The fact is that there is a constant stream of individual spirits becoming embodied, living out their life, and withdrawing again from the physical realm when their current body and its life have run their course.

This brings us to the next issue: How much does each individual contribute to and draw out of the experience of being embodied?

CHAPTER 7

The Self Seeks To Learn And Grow

C HAPTER TWO CONTAINED a proposition that human beings consist of a spiritual core consciousness residing in a body. This situation gives rise to inner depth, to self-awareness, and to being able to spiritually explore. In the previous chapter we further proposed that the self may be thought of as a labyrinth and that one needs a map to successfully explore the depths of the labyrinth that is the human self. The model of the five layered self has been presented to provide such a map.

We will now explore the implications that may be drawn from this model of the five-layered self. The aim is to illuminate how you may experience the depths of your own self, expand your self-awareness, and explore the inner possibilities you possess. All this is in order to learn, to achieve knowledge and, ultimately, to evolve as a spiritual identity. We'll begin by returning to the limitations of the everyday awareness.

THE PROBLEM OF HUMAN AWARENESS

Why are adult human beings not in touch with their core consciousness? Why is the normal adult human awareness not flooded with insights and illuminations emanating from its own spiritual self? This is the crux of human spirituality – or, more specifically, its absence from everyday human existence.

The proposal here is that all human beings possess, indeed each individual *is*, a spiritual core consciousness. But few are actively aware of the spiritual consciousness in their depths. In fact, large numbers of otherwise apparently sensitive and intelligent people are so unaware of their own spiritual consciousness that they actively deny it exists. Alternatively, if they do feel that it exists, they are unable to describe it. Why is this? In the last chapter we mentioned that fear is a significant deterrent. Many people are too scared to close their eyes and enter into their own self. There are also social deterrents, with many conditioned to think that meditation is too alternative, or outright hokum, or that mystical practices are part of the occult and are therefore suspect.

Within Christian circles the occult is widely viewed as being of the Devil. While some individuals involved in occult practices are decidedly up to no good, the truth is that the occult, like business, education and politics, is ethically neutral. Most fields of human endeavour are neither intrinsically good nor evil. They become positive or negative, nurturing or oppressive, freeing or coercive, depending on the attitudes of the individuals involved and what their motives are, whether they are driven by fear, selfishness, a search for knowledge, a need to find peace, a desire to help others, and so on.

It also needs to be made clear that the Devil is a human invention, being a projection of fear that some use to control others and that those others choose to absorb to inhibit themselves and to justify why they are limited to a narrow band of behaviours. Many use their fear of the Devil as a wall to hide behind, and to justify why they don't explore their inner selves.

It has to be added that the notion of original sin is part of this control/ inhibition mechanism. The Christian idea that human beings are intrinsically evil and that individuals just have to believe in God in order to be saved introduces two fundamental errors: that certain beliefs are fundamental to becoming spiritual, and that a supernatural being will save believers. Both are totally erroneous beliefs.

As we stated earlier, belief is not enough. You need to know. What we are further proposing in this chapter is that only you can do the work required to become knowing. No one else, no other being of any kind, is going to wave a wand over your spirit and enlighten it or transform you. As with every field of human endeavour, you gain mastery through sheer hard work. You become a concert pianist or a successful businessman by working hard at it. Similarly, you gain knowledge of your self, and not just theoretical knowledge, but practical knowledge that shows you how to navigate through the layers of your self and how to draw on and maximise the capacities latent within you, not by winning a spiritual lottery but by applying yourself.

So to repeat the question asked at the start of this section: Why are adult human beings not in touch with their spiritual core? The answer is that there are significant conditioning factors present in the everyday awareness that either stir up fear regarding the enterprise of spiritual exploration or that inhibit an individual's desire and ability should they wish to be adventurous. Accordingly, overcoming those limiting factors and confronting the assumptions discussed in Part One, is crucial to even starting out on a spiritual quest.

But where does this inhibition and fear ultimately rest? Not in the outside world. Why not? Because if you wish to you can always shrug off and rise above your social, religious or materialist conditioning. The fact is that the fear and inhibition rest within your layered self. You are the one who takes on board all the suggestions that are given to you. You are the one who selects from all the input you received during childhood and beyond. You are the one who has used what you have selected to construct your everyday identity. And you are the one who has the power to change what you think, feel, do, say and believe. Ultimately, no one else is responsible for your limitations. Or your strengths. It is entirely in your hands the degree to which you feel, think, act, and ultimately become, something new.

Because you are the filter for what you experience, or, to be more specific, because your externally conditioned and self-constructed everyday awareness is the filter for what you experience, becoming more sensitive to input from your spiritual self involves transforming how your everyday awareness functions. And because the everyday awareness is itself a function of how you function overall in your layered self, transforming the way your everyday awareness filters experiences involves transforming your layered self. Let's look at all this in more detail.

EXPLORATION, GROWTH AND SELF-TRANSFORMATION

Exploration and growth are linked. In fact, they are two aspects of the one activity. In order to perceive more spiritually you need to possess more capacity in your everyday awareness. And increasing that capacity involves making deeper parts of your layered self active, developing their functionality, and bringing them into daily life. But in order to develop anything you first have to discover that it is there. So initial exploration precedes growth. But then inner growth facilitates new exploration. Which leads to further inner growth. And so on.

This is why we are offering the model of the five-layered self: to help you discover your own inner nature, diminish false assumptions and fear, and to provide a map you may pragmatically use to explore.

Exploration and growth together provide the conditions for self transformation to occur. It is similar to working on a car engine. First the mechanic opens the hood and explores the engine in order to discover whether the spark plugs are firing correctly, if the timing is off, what faults may be inhibiting the engine's full functioning. Exactly the same occurs within the self. One has to lift the hood, have a look inside, see what is out of kilter, what isn't connected properly, what could be working better.

Of course, where the analogy breaks down is that an engine doesn't grow, doesn't evolve. Working on an engine makes it run more efficiently. But the engine has a maximum efficiency. However, after working under the hood of the self the result isn't just that the self functions more efficiently, with interactions between the various capacities operating at maximum capacity, even though that it is an admirable achievement in itself. The result of working on the self is that it grows. And the self has no maximal performance. Or, at least, performance is possible that far exceeds what you might imagine for yourself. Naturally, that is if you retain focus and put in the hard work.

To continue the analogy of the car engine, the reason a mechanic lifts the hood and explores the engine is either to service the engine or to locate and solve an issue that is impeding the car's maximal performance. Within the self we also need to service the layered self, in the sense of ensuring information flows between the various parts efficiently, identifying what impedes information flow, and adjusting, correcting or removing whatever is impeding that flow.

Hence the place where exploration initially occurs is in the everyday awareness. You have to become aware of the assumptions, attitudes, ideas, buffers, behaviours and conditioning that impede deep exploration. By becoming aware of them, appreciating how they came to be present, and dismantling those you don't need, you generate the possibility of exploring further.

To use another analogy, the exploration process is like entering a cave and discovering that passages leading deeper into the cave complex are blocked. Only after removing the rubble and clearing the passage may you progress. The same applies to exploring the inner self. Only by removing psychological rubble can you enter your own depths.

What you are doing when you clear psychological rubble is addressing and removing negative emotions and assumptions, self-limiting ideas and attitudes, and self-defensive buffers and behaviours. You are also dismantling the conditioning that has shaped your everyday identity. Subsequently, these negative, self-defensive and limiting factors are replaced by positive factors that enhance your life experiences and promote inner growth.

To be specific, clearing the psychological rubble accrued during childhood requires one first to identify negative emotions and then to replace them with positive qualities. To better appreciate how this process occurs, let's look at the example of a parent-child relationship.

AN EXAMPLE

Let's say that during your childhood your father repeatedly told you that you weren't good enough. And let's say he was projecting his own disappointment with himself onto you, his child. Such conditioning brought about in you a range of related attitudes and behaviours. Let's say that throughout your childhood you always doubted yourself. You felt you were inadequate and not up to successfully completing new challenges. So you played it safe, taking the easy option in order to avoid failing, avoiding new or challenging tasks whenever possible. Your self-esteem fell decidedly low. It even manifested in a rejection of reading books, because your father always read. You surreptitiously tried doing things your father didn't approve of, like smoking, to assert your own identity. But when your father found out that became another example of failing to measure up, of showing how inadequate, in his eyes, you always were.

Let's say further that you never addressed this childhood conditioning. Instead you covered it over, minimised contact with your father throughout your adult life, maybe by moving far away from him, and you got an easy and safe job. The truth is you actually now feel somewhat frustrated with your life. But addressing that frustration would involve digging up your feelings about your father, and you don't want to go there. So you keep the mat pulled over the emotional hole at the centre of your socialised identity. Then you have children of your own.

As your children grow up you decide you want them to have a better life than you feel you have had. You certainly don't want them to end up feeling inadequate and frustrated like you. So you encourage them to do well at school, to work hard at whatever they do, and to always put their best foot forward. Two children respond well. But the third child is tardy, is a little withdrawn, and doesn't make an effort like the others. This child becomes your favourite, because she reminds you of your own childhood self. In fact, she isn't tardy. She is just more naturally inclined to be introspective. But you become determined to help her get out of herself and engage with the world in the way you think she needs to be a success. Of course, what you are doing is projecting your own desired self-image onto her.

When she doesn't respond to your prodding and pushing as you think she should you start complaining to others about her poor attitude. Soon your natural well of frustration rises and you become short-tempered, even oppressive. How your daughter responds depends on her psychological make-up. She may emotionally withdraw. Or she may attempt to do what you require of her, but always fearing she will fail to measure up. The upshot is that what began as a nurturing impulse on your part, of pushing your child so she will do better in life than you feel you have, ends up with you inculcating the same feelings of inadequacy into her that you have yourself.

Projection is a big issue here. Why? Because it has stopped you seeing your daughter for what she actually is. All your children are individuals possessing their own potentials, goals and plans. And those may be quite different from yours. They may even be totally incompatible with what you see for them. So the expectations you project onto them don't necessarily reflect the reality of what they are. Hence what you do to help them ends up hindering them, just as your own father projected his disappointment with himself onto you. The only way to interrupt this cycle of projection is by facing up to your childhood conditioning, realising what in it has led to your negative feelings, and dismantling all that limits you.

This is clearing away psychological rubble. Only then are you able to enter a new "cave" within your layered self, where positive emotions reside. This deeper part of you is accepting, peaceful and entirely lacks your underlying anxiety of failure and inadequacy. If you were able to find and live from this emotional place, you would be able to communicate with your children without your childhood baggage getting in the way. Fundamentally, your efforts will have stimulated the growth of your emotions from anxiety to acceptance. As a result, you not only transform your own everyday emotional state, you also transform your relationship with your children.

To return to the analogy of the car, the emotional engine that drives your relationship with your children is now purring, and a far less fraught, more nurturing, more intimate and real relationship can then result. Of course, the nature of the relationship still depends on how your children respond. But that is another issue. The point is, you have cleared up your side of the relationship.

This is how exploration, transformation and growth are linked psychologically. The same process occurs in all other parts of the self. First you have to become aware of a blockage. Then you have to explore it, understand it, remove what is negative and limiting, and replace it with the positive and nurturing. Transformation of that particular part of the layered self results. And transformation leads to the growth of that part, which subsequently flows through into the everyday awareness. As a result, the way you perceive, experience, process and feel, think and act in your everyday life will also be transformed.

Much more will be stated about this process of self-transformation in the next two books, *Practical Spirituality* and *Psychological Spirituality*. For now we wish to comment further on growth. This first is that, as was stated earlier, much of this growth occurs within the essence self.

GROWTH AND THE ESSENCE SELF

The biological self follows a natural cycle of being born, growing, maturing into an adult, maintaining an adult level of functioning for a period, then of declining and eventually dying. This cycle may be cut short, but it cannot be altered. It is the cycle your core spiritual consciousness necessarily experiences within a human body.

The socialised self also changes over the course of a lifetime. One's self-image changes radically, reflecting the body's growth from infant to child to teen to adult to middle-aged to retired to dying. Social factors, such as success, being loved, being rejected, completing projects, not completing projects, being applauded or being ignored, all affect the self-image embedded in the socialised self, sometimes tremendously. But these changes in the socialised self are not growth. They merely reflect changes in social environment and in how an individual feels in relation to being in that environment.

Accordingly, it may be stated categorically that human growth occurs within the essence self. Four points follow from this.

It is only in the essence self that real growth occurs. This growth is moving, emotional and intellectual. One can be infantile in the functioning in one of these capacities. Or adult. While the precise gradations from infant to adult growth can be made, they would be arbitrary, as this framework is offered to provide a general idea of growth. Furthermore, while we are referring to moving, emotional and intellectual growth, these are certainly not the only indicators of development one could use. One could equally say there is moral development, social development, artistic development, parenting development, or leadership development. However, it could also be said that all these various capacities exist in the essence self and draw on the moving, emotional and intellectual capacities inherent in the human cognitive functions. So the basic point stands: that however growth is demarcated, the development of learned skills, of natural abilities, and of beyond-the-norm talents, all occur in the essence self.

Essence talents are to be nurtured. We have spent several pages referring to the need to overcome negative and self-limiting factors in order to grow. We need to balance that emphasis on "struggling against" by now emphasising the fact that each individual has particular talents present in their essence self that life situations offer the opportunity to nurture. Some talents are genetically inherited, some are not genetically present bvut are brought in by the spiritual self in order to be worked on and developed in this life. In everyday life much attention is paid to and applause given to individuals whose talents have led to success in some field of endeavour. In fact, everyone has talents. And there is no need to link talents to worldly success. It is through nurturing your own talents that much that makes you happiest – even blissful – in your life occurs. This is because talents are manifestations of drives and traits that ultimately emanate from your spiritual self, but that manifest at the essence level. Their expression in your life is helped or hindered by attitudes embedded in your socialised self. Doubts and fears stop many people from fully expressing their essence talents. This is another reason why addressing your negativities and self-limiting traits is necessary – because they are stopping you from being all you have the capacity to be and from achieving deep happiness and bliss.

A new essence balance needs to be established. Another factor that differentiates individuals, a factor that leads to each individual being unique, is the different balances that occur between the various parts of the layered self. We have already commented that within the essence self some individuals have a predilection for, and naturally give more of their everyday awareness over to, experiencing predominantly via one of their moving, emotional or intellectual capacities. We noted that individuals may be an infant or a child or an adult in their moving, emotional or intellectual capacities. So one person may be adult in their moving capacity, a child in their emotional capacity, and an infant in their intellectual capacity. Or the opposite. Given the variety of balances that are possible between the three capacities, and adding in differences in, for example, moral, artistic, social, parenting and leadership awareness and skills, there is a huge range of developmental possibilities within the essence parts of the self. All this does not preclude an individual being adult in all three capacities. However, that is far from common. As a result, everyone has considerable work to do at the essence level of their self.

Creating balance within the everyday awareness. The balance between the five layers of the self also needs to be addressed. Individuals begin their cycle of incarnations on this planet with zero awareness of their spiritual self. That is, in their everyday awareness they are not conscious that they are a spiritual being. Copnversely, after they have lived through their full cycle of incarnations they are very conscious, within their everyday awareness, that they are a spiritual being. The growth in this consciousness of intrinsically being a spiritual identity may be characterised as spiritual growth from infant to adult. This is the overall object of embodiment and of growth: to become aware, within the everyday awareness, of one's spiritual capacity. This is the spiritual mastery that is the goal of incarnating as a human being.

But, of course, just as one does not gain mastery over the concert piano in one stroke, but must work at it over an extended period, so one does not gain spiritual mastery in one stroke. It occurs as a result of focused effort over an extended period of time. Lifetimes, in fact.

GROWTH IS INTRINSIC

As an aside, we would comment on an assumption that is frequently made in some spiritual circles. This is that gaining spiritual mastery occurs at a stroke, as a result of a single enlightenment experience. This is not true. Anyone can certainly have an "ah-ha" moment, in which insight clicks into place, whether temporarily or permanently. But there is no single enlightenment event.

If we envisage spiritual mastery as standing at the peak of a mountain, no one is ever magically transported from the bottom of a valley, or from halfway up a hillside, to the top of the mountain. One gets to the mountain peak by climbing. And when one arrives there one then sees something one hadn't previously observed. This being that there are other much higher mountains that are now accessible to continued climbing.

All this should not stimulate a negative feeling of futility, or cause you to wonder what is the point if there is an apparently never-ending process involved. Neither should anyone conclude that they should hunker down wherever they are and not bother to make an effort, that it's all the same wherever one is and whatever one does. The fact is there are mind-boggling vistas to be perceived, tremendous opportunities to explore. You yourself possess capacities of which you are totally unaware. And even within this human existence you are capable of levels of experience, growth and self-transformation that are inconceivable to your current everyday awareness.

You also have an obligation to your own spiritual self to work against emotional negativities and psychological limitations, to nurture your talents, and to make the most of the opportunities you have in your life. Why? Because this is why you, as a spiritual identity, sought to be born into the body and life you have – to experience, to learn and to grow. So choosing to hunker down and just live out your life where you are, making minimal effort, is actually contrary to your own long-term interests. It is contrary to why you chose to be embodied in the first place.

Hence it could be said that avoiding making an effort is another example of the self-defensive behaviour of the everyday awareness. In this case, it is an awareness dominated by the fear-filled socialised self, which happily hunkers down where it is in an effort to avoid being challenged, tested or moved away from where it thinks it is safe. This hunkering down is akin to an ostrich placing its head in the sand in the middle of a veldt teeming with other animals. And the danger is not necessarily one of being eaten by predators. The danger is that all the other animals migrate to new pastures, and the ostrich is left all alone and in danger of starving to death.

Of course, this is all metaphorical. The spiritual self can never die. But it can be poorly or well nourished. And it may or may not achieve the full potential of what it could become. As parents well know, food feeds growth. On the spiritual level, experiences provide food. So anyone who avoids new experiences, new challenges and new tests impedes their own growth.

Everything in the universe is evolving. The growth urge surges within all life. But we each also have choice. Anyone can choose to eat and so grow. Or to eat little and not grow to the extent of which they are capable.

CHAPTER 8

Beliefs Facilitate
Or Impede Growth

HAVING IDENTIFIED GROWTH as intrinsic to humanity, we will now consider how beliefs impact on growth. Beliefs fall into one of two fundamental categories: beliefs that facilitate growth and beliefs that impede
growth. Two examples will indicate how each of these categories works in
practice.

In 1911 Ernest Rutherford drew on data he had derived from testing
gold to propose a new model of the atom. This hypothetical model proposed
that the atom consisted of a nucleus circled by a cloud of orbiting electrons.
However, other scientists, assuming that Newtonian physics applied at the
sub-atomic level, objected that any orbiting object, such as an electron, would
lose energy and eventually fall into the nucleus. This meant the model predicted all matter was inherently unstable, which was clearly not the case.
To resolve this problem Neils Bohr adjusted the model by proposing that
electrons orbited the nucleus in strict valances or levels, and that electrons
could only leave that level in special circumstances. This became the Rutherford-Bohr model which, with its electrons circling the nucleus like planets,
is today the classic image of the atom.

But atomic-level effects and behaviours were still observed that this new
model could not account for. Like Copernicus before him, Bohr had assumed
that electrons orbited the nucleus in circles. Experimentally obtained data
contradicted the circle hypothesis. The problem was resolved when Arnold
Sommerfeld proposed that electrons orbit the nucleus in elliptical paths.
The accepted understanding of the atom now became the Sommerfeld-Bohr

model. Yet there still remained anomalous data that was inconsistent with the model.

This issue was only resolved in 1926 when a new quantum model of the atom was developed by Erwin Schrödinger using mathematics generated by Wolfgang Pauli and Werner Heisenberg. This new model proposed that electrons were not like mini-planets circling the nucleus, but were better described as packets of energy (quanta). Furthermore, these energy packets didn't conform to the predictive equations of classical Newtonian physics but were better understood using probability equations. This is largely the model of the atom that is preferred by physicists today.

It can be seen from this that Rutherford's initial model, which was built on previous data and theories, was an incorrect hypothesis. However, his proposed model was not a failure. Far from it. It offered a new way of thinking about the atom that stimulated other physicists to think beyond the previously assumed truths. The end result was that, after trialling various concepts, and building on prior discoveries, a small group of physicists progressively arrived at the currently accepted quantum model of the atom.

In the context of this discussion, that example shows how a belief, which in scientific terms is a hypothesis, facilitates the growth of knowledge. Indeed, while the Rutherford-Bohr model does not strictly conform to reality, it is still taught to students of physics today as a useful introduction.

An example of a belief that impedes growth is provided by what occurred when Paleolithic cave paintings were first discovered in 1879 in Altamira, by Marcelino de Sautuola's nine year old daughter. Sautuola was a farmer and amateur archeologist. Working with an academic archeologist, Professor Juan Vilanova y Piera, Sautuola published a book on the paintings the following year in which together they proposed the paintings were by Paleolithic hunter-gatherers, dating back thousands of years.

The public were enthused by the find. But the experts of the day, led by French academics Louis Laurent Gabriel de Mortillet and Émile Cartailhac, rejected the discovery. Their rationale was that the paintings were of high artistic quality. But they assumed that Paleolithic hunter-gatherers were not sufficiently intelligent to produce paintings of such quality. So they asserted that the paintings were actually modern. Cartailhac then accused Sautola of forgery. Only in 1902, when paintings had been discovered in other caves in Spain and France, did Cartailhac backtrack and admit he was in error. In the meantime Sautola had died and Professor Juan Vilanova y Piera's professional reputation and career had been ruined.

This is not only example of the way that belief impedes growth, it is also an example of the way that the socialised self's desire to maintain its status interfered with the proper activity of the essence self's intellect. The result was that Cartailhac didn't treat the discovery as revealing fascinating new data and use his intellect to evaluate it. Instead, he used his intellect to dismiss the discovery and defend his own assumed beliefs. What drove his behaviour was his desire to maintain his academic status and social position. This outweighed his essence self's desire to know. As a result, scientific progress was impeded. In this particular case progress was only impeded for twenty years. But two careers were ruined in the process.

This is not only an example of how beliefs impede growth. It also shows what occurs when beliefs become entangled in defensive behaviours and are used as psychological weapons to defend, defeat and control. Accordingly, we need to examine the psychology of belief.

THE PSYCHOLOGY OF BELIEF

No beliefs exist in a vacuum. It could be said that beliefs form a subset of the full range of human meaning-making. The result is that all those factors that play into the construction of meaning also play into beliefs. Thus tradition, cultural acceptance and social norms impact significantly on what people believe. In simple terms, people tend to believe what everyone else around them believes. This is human nature, explained by the fact that humanity is a social species that survives and grows best in groups rather than individually.

However, while the degree to which cultural inputs structure shared beliefs is widely appreciated, the reasons people continue to give credence to beliefs, especially when the usefulness and appropriateness of those beliefs has long run its course, is much less widely understood. This psychological aspect needs to be considered.

Fundamentally, beliefs are sustained through the agency of the human psychological make-up. That is, no matter what the actual source of any belief, it is individuals, and masses of individuals believing together, who sustain any belief. If no one accepted a particular belief then it would simply fade away. As noted earlier, beliefs are generated by and are sustained in the everyday awareness. So when the everyday awareness ceases to sustain a belief, that belief ceases to exist. This occurs on both the mass and individual levels.

Throughout human history there have been innumerable beliefs that were invented by and sustained in the human everyday awareness, then dropped when the general outlook changed. A belief in a flat Earth is an example. This was believed fervently by millions, to the extent that when Christopher Columbus set sail from Spain for the Indies there was a popular belief that his ship would sail off the edge of the world. Columbus didn't consider his ship was in danger because he had maps that showed lands to the west of Europe. He had knowledge that contradicted popular belief. Of course, today all laugh at such a belief. Yet there are beliefs that are fervently sustained today that will prove equally laughable in future centuries.

The psychological trait that leads people to sustain beliefs when fresh knowledge has shown them to be erroneous is defensiveness. In the case of the Altamira cave paintings, the experts rejected new data in favour of continuing their belief. Why? In that case because they wished to defend their academic status and their related social positions. The academics even played dirty to defend their socialised selves. Denying the evidence, they withheld data from peer reviewers and attacked the characters of Sautuola and Piera. This is psychologically and not scientifically motivated behaviour.

Self-defensiveness manifests in the behaviours of denying, justifying, deflecting and attacking. These behaviours are freely utilised in the defense of publicly-held beliefs. In the sphere of religion people have been ostracised for not believing as they should, had their characters besmirched, been cast out from their communities, have been beaten emotionally and physically, and been tortured and even murdered. In the halls of academia those who espouse beliefs that are too far from the mainstream, or who have ventured into research areas that are considered unacceptable, have been ostracised, had their characters besmirched, or been refused publication in peer review journals.

Such situations are examples of how humanity's natural tendency towards social cohesion, which has led to great cultural, scientific, technological, intellectual and even moral progress, descends into primitive pack behaviour when people feel they need to defend "their" territory and see off anyone who threatens the status quo. It can be appreciated that behind such self-defensive behaviours is the root emotion of fear.

Fear comes in many forms. Fear of the stranger. Fear of the new. Fear of the unknown. Fear of dying. Fear of losing those one holds dear. Fear of losing what one knows. Fear of losing the comfort of being what one is.

As was observed earlier, ultimately fear can be traced back to the fear of being a new spiritual core consciousness existing in a huge and unknown reality. This existential fear then joins with the animal fear mechanism associated with the old brain's flight or flight mechanism. Together, these two levels of fear then coalesce in the everyday awareness. As we also stated earlier, defensive behaviours have developed historically within all human cultures as a way of coping with shared fears and keeping them at bay.

One example already referred to is the belief that it is necessary to offer prayers and sacrifices to a harsh and vengeful God in order to prevent horrible things happening to the tribe, village or family. Another example is the belief that if strangers has given the opportunity they will take what one has, so they must be kept away. A current example is the belief in the West that terrorists wish to disrupt everyone's way of life, a fear which has given rise to a wide range of self-defensive behaviours, with governments now openly spying on their citizens and some people advocating that everyone should be armed.

Of course, many individuals exploit others' fears to further their own goals. This tension between those who believe to compensate for their fear, and those who use the opportunity provided by that fear to further their own interests, has been well documented. Whether through acquiescence or manipulation, fear-fuelled beliefs have had a significant impact on human culture through the ages. And continue to do so.

This brings us to a consideration of the relationship between beliefs and identity.

IDENTITY AND BELIEF

A key psychological factor that leads people to hold onto their beliefs, despite their beliefs having been shown to be invalid, is because those beliefs underpin their identity. As we noted earlier, identity is complex. It functions on multiple levels simultaneously.

First and deepest is spiritual identity. The spiritual identity has no need for beliefs of any kind. It deals directly with spiritual level perceptions in which what is real to the individual is the sole criteria. Similarly, the body deals directly with physical sense perceptions and has no need of beliefs. No animals use or need beliefs. All animals function only on sense experience and what their memory of previous experiences tells them.

So if beliefs are not required by identity at the spiritual and biological levels, where do beliefs exist? At the level of the human socialised self and within everyday awareness. This is where beliefs arise and are maintained. In contrast, it is at the level of the essence self that beliefs are tested for validity and adopted as knowledge or rejected as invalid.

In order to appreciate the way that beliefs are conditioned into each human identity via the socialised self, and are subsequently tested and evaluated by the essence self, it is necessary to briefly appraise how human identity is constructed.

As observed earlier, the natural animal drives and desires of the human biological self were socialised long ago. Thus lust was socialised into marriage, reproduction was socialised into the family (allowing that family structures take very different forms in different cultures), and the biological drives to obtain food and shelter were socialised into work, paydays, bank accounts, credit cards, paying tax, supermarkets, home handyman stores, and so on. The interactions of multiple similarly conditioned socalised selves gives each human culture its basic flavour, attitudes, approach to living, and conduits for communication and expression.

This socialisation of biological drives provides one level of identity, seen in the way that people say of another that they are a fussy eater, or a good worker, or a snappy dresser, or an entertaining talker, and so on. Social level identity also derives from schooling, occupation, family, social status, hobbies and interests, along with the places you frequent and the people you spend most time with. All these factors, and too many others to list, feed into each person's combined physical and social identity.

The next level of identity is at the level of the essence self. This is the level of identity that seeks to learn, to improve, to grow. In contrast, the biological self seeks to survive and to satisfy its animal desires, and the socialised self seeks to accommodate itself to the social environment in which it lives and to the groups and individuals who live there with it. Only the identity at the essence level strives to experience, absorb, learn and gain mastery.

Negative and limiting traits are certainly present within the essence self. These psychological traits can also latch onto beliefs and use them defensively. We will examine this process in *Psychological Spirituality*. Nonetheless, for now, and as a general statement, it can be said that beliefs are of no use to identity at the level of the biological self, are used defensively by the socialised self, are questioned by the essence self, absolutely do not connect with the aura at the level of the energetic self, and are waded through during the course of a life by the spiritual self as it strives to achieve its life goals.

Accordingly, it can be seen that the process of challenging and evaluating one's beliefs is a task that involves the essence self, and principally the intellect of the essence self, in which it weighs and tests beliefs held by the socialised self. This explains why challenging long inculcated beliefs can be so fraught with high emotion – because it involves one part of your identity critiquing and challenging another part. In effect, you are challenging beliefs that underpin who you have been conditioned to think you are.

This is also why, when others critique your beliefs, it usually feels that they are attacking you personally – because those beliefs are firmly lodged in your socialised self and manifest naturally as part of your everyday awareness. So when they attack your beliefs you feel they are attacking you. And what is the natural psychological response? To defend yourself by denying, justifying, deflecting or attacking. Once the criticism is seen off, you pull the mat back over the hole at the centre of your socialised identity and carry on.

But what if the criticism strikes home? What if, instead of automatically defending yourself, you stop your inner reactions, listen to what is said, and take it on board? What in you responds in this way? The answer is, your essence self. Your essence self facilitates learning from experience. It is the part of your identity that hears the criticism and takes it on board.

In contrast, once the socialised self has adjusted itself to its social environment, which in the normally functioning individual occurs by adulthood, it has no interest in further learning and growing. It doesn't need to. At best it makes minor behavioural adjustments in response to changes in its local environment in order to better fit in. That is all.

So to facilitate personal growth each individual needs to develop a self-image, situated in their everyday awareness, that shifts from mere social-level accommodation to an identity that is committed to essence-level learning and growing. Doing so will also facilitate the process of eliminating beliefs that are no longer required and that impede personal growth, even though those beliefs underpin the socialised self's self-image.

Only the essence self is capable of treating beliefs as propositions. Hence we return to the examples with which we began this chapter. The socialised self wields beliefs defensively, to protect its social identity, and as a consequence closes down exploration. In contrast, the essence self is able to perceive beliefs as propositions and use them to open up new territory and knowledge. In the process, the essence self facilitates self-transformation and growth.

BELIEFS AS TOOLS

From all this it can be seen that beliefs are really only tools. Throughout history human beings have always sought to understand what is happening around them. Initially they told stories, an activity that occupies every single human being alive. These are stories about what happened, what didn't happen, what people would like to happen, what has happened to others, what they wish hadn't happened, what was apparently always going to happen. Story-telling, whether it involves recounting them or listening to them being told, has always occupied the human everyday awareness from the first moment of the day to the last.

Over time, ambitious individuals started telling stories that were more elaborate than the norm. Some of these stories were enjoyed by others and as a result were repeated, orally or in written form. These stories eventually became fairy tales, tales of the supernatural, myths, religious narratives, and origin stories about a people, a nation or the entire universe. Subsequently, beliefs were extracted from these stories. And these beliefs were adopted as truths that tell how the world is.

An example is provided by the current fad for vampire stories. The roots of stories of the undead goes back to ancient times, being a manifestation of the fear of the unknown in general and of the state of death in particular. The recent English language fad for vampire folklore stems first from Victorian novelists then from the cinema. Vampires are mythically said to have originated from Transylvania where Count Dracula, the leading character of the modern vampire myth, supposedly lived. But among Russian Christians there was an alternative belief that those who were heretics or apostates from the Russian Orthodox Church were candidates for becoming vampires. And in other cultures the belief was that if an animal jumped over a corpse it would rise as a vampire.

Of course, this is all poppycock. The entire vampire lore merely reflects the human love of a good story, especially one that scares them silly. For most people such stories are purely entertainment. Others respond to them, whether consciously or unconsciously, as expressions of their own deep-seated fear of death. Yet others view such stories as an opportunity to cash in and make money. For a tiny minority such stories even fuel an actual belief in vampires. Such is the diversity of human psychology.

The point being made here is not that such story-telling is wrong. Or even that it is unnecessary. Indeed, the opposite is the case, because story-telling is a vital part of absorbing experiences and generating meaning from them. Rather, the point is that beliefs are just one tool in the complete toolkit of human meaning-making. Just as story-telling is a tool. And experimenting is a tool. And reading books. And talking to people about your deepest hopes. And seeking out new experiences and perspectives. However, as with any tool, there is a proper way of using belief and an improper way – given that proper use facilitates growth and improper use impedes growth.

We have commented at length on improper ways that beliefs are used. We will now consider the proper use of beliefs.

FOUR APPLICATIONS

CHAPTER 9

The Significance
Of New Data

EVERYONE WHO ENGAGES in a spiritual quest expects a significant pay-off. Perhaps they want to be transported out of themselves into the divine. Or to have extraordinary visions. Or experience ecstasy. Or receive extraordinary revelations. Unfortunately, the reality of the spiritual search, particularly in its initial phases, is much more humdrum than these excited expectations suggest.

The fact is that before you can arrive at the mountaintop and see the world that lies beyond the peak, you have to climb out of the valley in which you currently live. And before you can even begin climbing you need to appreciate your situation. You need to become clear about where you are and what path you need to follow. You also need to appreciate what is holding you back. Doing this last task involves looking not only at what is humdrum but at what is decidedly unappetising.

Another Greek myth provides an insight into what is required to successfully engage in your own spiritual quest. The story goes that after being driven mad by the goddess Hera the Greek hero Herakles killed his six sons. After he returned to sanity he was required to complete ten labours in order to repay for his actions. One of these labours involved cleaning out the Augean stables in a single day. What made this task so challenging was that the cattle numbered one thousand, and being divine they produced prodigious amounts of excrement. Moreover, the stables had not been cleaned for thirty years.

To adjust this myth to the current context, before you can leave where you currently live – and we are referring not to your street address but to your inner psycho-spiritual state – you need to clean out the stables of your self. The ordure inside you consists of negativities and self-limiting attitudes and behaviours that have built up over the course of your life, and beyond. They now gum up your perceptions and prevent you striding out into a spiritually-imbued future.

The reason the spiritual quest begins with what is not merely humdrum, but with what is distinctly unappetising, is that dealing with what is negative and self-limiting is like shovelling ordure. But the task is unavoidable because they are what prevents you from stepping out of your current self into a new transformed self and perspective. The key to identifying this psychological ordure is obtaining new data. Specifically, new data about your self.

THE POINT OF NEW DATA

Everyone is acclimatised to what they are. During the course of growing up everyone undergoes negative experiences, perhaps even traumatic experiences, that hinder the expression of their essence traits. Everyone develops defense mechanisms for coping with life situations, starting with the home and expanding to peers and the wider community. And everyone has fears they have covered over and suppressed using any of the vast array of behavioural strategies that manifest via the human socialised self. All this constitutes the "excrement" that is piled up within the layered self.

But even worse than having one's perceptions "gummed up by excrement" is that each person learns to become comfortable with their particular excrement and its stink. Technically, we call this state "being acclimatised to crystallised everyday identity". This is the psychological state of the normal adult human being has reached by the nominal age of twenty-one.

Everyday identity is crystallised in the sense that. within the psychological makeup, a comfortable accommodation has been formed with a particular variety of repressed fear, and that accommodation enables the individual to function in the world without generating unbearable emotional tensions and without impinging extremely on others. The result of living in this crystallised state is that everyone domesticates their particular brand of psychological excrement. They make it familiar. They even identify with it, saying:

This is the way I am, this is my nature. And they view the world through a perceptual mechanism tinted, in fact tainted, by their individualised brand of excrement.

We have previously commented on how people defend this pile of excrement when they are criticised by others. Why do so? Because each identifies with their particular crystallised pattern of behaviours as constituting who and what they are. Of course, this is not who or what they are at all. This is just a collection of conditioned behaviours arrayed around a central fear. On the spiritual level they are a spiritual identity who soars far above this stable filled with ordure. And even on the human level they exist in their essence self as a significantly different array of talent and feelings, thoughts and actions, which contribute to a wholly alternative form of self-identity.

Unfortunately, due to perception being gummed up, individuals don't see even this alternative essence self. What do they need in order to see it? They need to see themselves differently. And to do that they need new data about themselves that provides an alternative perspective on who and what they are and on why and how their life is the way it is. But being open to receiving new data about oneself is no easily achieved task.

THE DIFFICULTY OF RECEIVING NEW DATA

In order to receive new data about your self all the defense mechanisms that have crystallised around your central fear need to be by-passed.

It might be thought that the young automatically have an advantage over the older in accepting new data, because their defensive behaviours are not as crystallised and have not been locked into place for years, as is the case with older individuals. This is not so.

The key to being receptive to new data about yourself and the world around you is the degree to which your spiritual self manages to make itself heard at the level of your everyday awareness. And your spiritual self usually organises this to occur at a particular stage of your life journey.

For some there is a plan to engage with the spiritual's self's manifestation within the everyday awareness at a young age. For others the plan is to do so at a later stage, after other preliminary tasks have been completed.

As a result, for some the spiritual self may, over a period of years, stimulate emotions of unhappiness or dissatisfaction or even disgust with life circumstances, all in preparation for opening up the individual to new data. For others receptiveness may occur as a result of processing traumatic life events that were themselves prepared for prior to birth.

There are actually many different circumstances that lead to individuals becoming receptive to new data about themselves, too numerous to list. What they have in common is that each is an instance of an individual's spiritual self preparing the inner ground for the successful reception of new data.

This brings us to an interesting line of thought, for there are two distinct perspectives on what occurs during this process. There is the spiritual self's perspective. And there is the perspective of the everyday identity.

The spiritual self views the everyday identity as a sub-identity of itself. During the course of each incarnation the spiritual self inhabits a body, and that body has a unique sub-identity associated with it. As a result your spiritual self has incarnated within a series of bodies and their associated sub-identities. You are no more – and no less – than the latest of these sub-identities. In addition, prior to each life your spiritual self sets itself a number of goals it wishes to achieve, using that particular sub-identity and its body to do so. So it needs to communicate with its sub-identity in order to fulfil those goals. It may do so overtly or covertly, without the sub-identity being consciously aware of that communication within its everyday awareness, or alternatively by making its requirements very clearly felt.

You, the reader of this book, having reached this far through the text, may consider that your spiritual self is using this text to alert you, at the level of your everyday awareness, to its presence in order to convey new data to you about what it requires in order to satisfactorily fulfil its goals. To "get the message through" the spiritual self needs its current sub-identity to stop living wholly in its socially conditioned identity and to begin to consciously and deliberately engage in its essence level goals. In order to do this, the spiritual self needs to place new data in the sub-identity's everyday awareness. The point of this new data is to wake up the sub-identity to alternative possibilities. In this way the life trajectory will be shifted from being aligned with the desires and fears of the socialised self to being aligned with the spiritual self's goals as they manifest within the essence self. This is the human situation from the persepctive of the spiritual self. We'll now examine the same situation from the perspective of everyday identity.

For an individual living at the level of everyday identity, which is necessarily focused on the activities of the body and of the socialised self, the arrival of new data can be confusing, even disconcerting. Why? Because the everyday identity doesn't know where this new data has come from. The spiritual domain is unknown to it. And even if the socialised self has generated a self-image that incorporates religious or spiritual ideas and impulses, the complete change in perspective that the spiritual self generates, (using whatever emotional, intellectual or moving means it has at its disposal within the individual's makeup, which it considers will most effectively impinge on the everyday awareness), means the individual experiences this stimulation as a conundrum. The conundrum not only involves the question of where this new data is coming from, but also what it signifies. Then there is the crucial question, what should be done with this new data?

Of course, few people consciously articulate this conundrum with such clarity. For most it exists, as we have said, as an unease, as discomfort, or as a profound dissatisfaction with their life. So for most people the conundrum manifests emotionally. For some it triggers a mid-life crisis. For others it causes them to lose their appetite, to become short-tempered, to feel their accustomed view of life is under threat. For some it may present as a relationship, occupational, ethical or intellectual dilemma, the solution to which requires them to open themselves up to a completely new way of proceeding in their life.

There are two principal responses to this impingement manifesting from the spiritual self into everyday awareness. The first is to repress it, self-calm, and carry on as before. The second is to accept it, embrace it, and use it to transform your life.

NEW DATA AND ASSUMPTIONS

The psycho-spiritual jolt that results when new data impinges on your everyday awareness is crucial to your awareness breaking out of the limits imposed on it by the crystallised socialised self. It is crucial to waking you up to your plight of living knee-high in ordure and to you becoming aware that you need to get rid of the ordure in order to align your life trajectory with your spiritual self's goals. This makes new data crucial to preparing the ground for self-transformation and growth.

New data actually surrounds everyone all the time. Whether this is data about climate change, new work possibilities, or even observations others make about your behaviour, there is no shortage of material that offers you new ways of viewing either the world or yourself. The question is, are you willing to receive it?

We have spent some time indicating that what prevents most people from receiving new data is their assumptions. Everyone assumes certain things about themselves, about the world, about God, about other people, about what is true and is not true. Most people also have firm ideas regarding what is most meaningful to them. So when they come across new ideas regarding human spiritual existence they weigh these ideas against what they already know, and they accept or reject them accordingly. As we have attempted to make clear, assumptions exist in the everyday awareness. And the everyday awareness is limited. An example will help clarify this further.

Let's say there are two individuals. The first is actually quite experientially knowing on the level of her spiritual self. But she is unable to articulate what she knows via her everyday awareness. In contrast, the second individual considers, at the level of her everyday awareness, that her thinking and feeling is very much in alignment with her spiritual self. Yet, because she is not spiritually aware, she is quite wrong. So both individuals have a disjunct between their spiritual self and their everyday awareness. The difference between them is that the first is actually spiritually knowing while the second is not.

If each of these two individuals then received new data regarding their spiritual nature, data in the form of words, at the level of their everyday awareness both would likely be shocked. Why? Because they are being presented with material they hadn't previously considered. But after the initial shock had died away, if they then decided to process the data, each would do so quite differently.

The first would have to grapple with new ways of thinking about spirituality, most likely involving new terminology. She would initially be puzzled as to how to reconcile the new words with what she has previously experienced. But after a period of grappling with the data she would see that, while it offers a new way of thinking about things spiritual, it is actually in sync with her own prior experiences. Indeed, given sufficiently serious consideration, she will find this new data articulates her experiences well. And so she will gradually digest the new data into her everyday awareness. The result is that she will now be able to consciously articulate experiences that she previously was unable to explain.

In contrast, the second individual needs to set aside what she thinks she knows in order to be open to receiving the new data and learning from it. Doing that requires her to address her assumptions about what spirituality is and what she is as a spiritual identity. She will also have to address the fears that feed her assumptions. Only then will she will be able to absorb the new data in a meaningful way. If she automatically rejects the data, on whatever grounds, then the possibility of a new inner alignment is stopped dead. (We view those who respond to the data by saying Yes!, without weighing it up, as not being sufficiently serious. More is written on this in the next chapter.)

This book is, from the perspective of the spiritual self, an attempt to offer new data to all those who come across it. We have deliberately made a number of assertions without attempting to argue for their validity. We have presented them as facts from the spiritual domain. From the perspective of your everyday awareness this data is likely anomalous. That is, there are likely to be statements that have struck you, the reader, as interesting, but at the same time they don't fit either with what you know or with the assumed truths by which you live. Some statements may even have attracted your attention on the grounds that they are preposterous or impossible. This jarring with your current sensibility is what makes statements or data anomalous.

From the scientific perspective, anomalous data is always interesting because it offers a direction for discovering new things about the world. From the spiritual perspective, anomalous data is new data that challenges your established view of the world and of yourself. But instead of rejecting this anomalous data out of hand, we suggest you use it to stimulate a new line of research into an aspect of your existence.

We hope that you have found the preceding chapters contain at least some anomalous data, and that this data will stimulate you to lift your feet out of the ordure of the everyday, and to shovel away enough to form a path by which you may start trekking into the unknown.

The following chapter explores how a spiritual enquiry might proceed.

CHAPTER 10

Asking Questions
In The Right Way

THE NEXT ISSUE IS WHAT to do with new data when you receive it. What kind of questions should you use it to ask? And is there a right way and wrong way of asking? This last question is significant because anyone may enquire into the nature of their existence. Yet it is not the case that everyone arrives at useful answers. This is because getting answers is not just a matter of being open to new data and using your openness to fire questions about whatever intrigues you. Obtaining useful answers also depends on the context in which a question is asked. And on asking in a way that leads to fruitful results.

Regarding the overall context in which questions are formulated and data is received, that context consists of your own life experiences. To reiterate the premise asserted in Part One, you are a spiritual identity. You have entered a chosen human body and you are currently experiencing a life via the capacities available within that body. In one sense, every endeavour you engage in, every exploration you make – whether it involves an everyday activity such as farming or building or playing music or digging ditches, or involves an overtly spiritual activity such as meditation – can be classed as spiritual. This is because at your core you are a spiritual identity. Therefore whatever you do is an expression of that identity.

To bring this discussion down to a crass level, does this mean that idly picking your nose while stopped at traffic lights is a spiritual endeavour? No. That is a self-cleaning activity on the body level. But if the nose picking was by a doctor gathering tissue for a diagnosis, and if the doctor had become a doctor as an expression of the qualities present at the essence and spiritual levels, then yes, nose picking is a spiritual endeavour. Intention distinguishes between activities that, on the one hand, are animal or social activities and, on the other, those that have a spiritual dimension.

INTENTION AND BEING MOTIVATED

Being motived requires conscious engagement and intention. Living unthinkingly and stupidly, without caring for others and without nurturing your own inner capacities, is not a consciously spiritual existence, even though it involves a spirit living inside a body.

Spirituality is an activity that requires sustained motivation. Furthermore, that motivation is generated by, and derives from the intention of, the spiritual identity. When any spirit enters a human body it intends to experience, learn, grow, gain mastery, and evolve as a spiritual identity. This intention equally applies to spirits in their non-embodied existence, for this is always the intention of all spiritual beings.

However, while this is the *intention* of all spirits, it is also true that not all embodied spirits are equally *motivated* during the course of their life. There are occasions when individuals become depressed, wonder what they are doing here living this life, become resentful, or angry, or self-pitying, and lose their way. By "losing their way" we mean that in their everyday awareness they lose their connection with their spiritual self. As a result they don't take up the tasks, or perhaps even cease doing those tasks they have already begun, that the spiritual self set itself to achieve during this life journey.

Equally, there are other times when that very same individual picks up him or herself, reconnects with spiritual-level aims, refocuses on the tasks at hand, and becomes highly motivated to carry out what has been chosen. It is not that the spiritual self's intention went away. It is that the individual, at the level of their everyday awareness, departed from that intention. So while intention is always present with equal intensity, motivation waxes and wanes. And so the degree to which a life may be labelled consciously spiritual, unconsciously spiritual, or not overtly or covertly spiritual at all, correspondingly waxes and wanes.

Accordingly, in order to use anomalous data you have received to begin an enquiry into a particular aspect of your existence, being motivated is key. And, to expand on what was stated above, being motivated depends on maintaining a *sustained engagement* with the intention that emanates from your spiritual self – an intention that selected, prepared for, and initiated the circumstances of your life so it might achieve its self-chosen goals.

We emphasised the words *sustained engagement* in the above paragraph because without continued effort over an extended period of time little will be achieved. As with any other kind of human endeavour, what you get out of spiritual exploration is a direct function of how much time, effort and energy you put in.

Having made clear that the initial condition of motivation is required to set out on any kind of exploration, let's clarify how an investigation into any aspect of your spiritual existence may best be carried out.

BEGINNING A SPIRITUAL ENQUIRY

At the outset it needs to be made clear that there are two fundamental kinds of enquiries. The first is an enquiry into the circumstances of your daily existence. This can extend from enquiring into your own psychological makeup, to seeking to understand another person's psychological make-up, to enquiring into the way something in the world functions on either the physical or extra-physical levels, to attempting to arrive at the most humane and ethical decision in a complex situation.

Any externally directed enquiry which has an intent of looking beyond the surface of things may be considered to have a spiritual impulse. Why? Because, as was stated earlier, the human animal doesn't need to be ethical, doesn't need to understand its own psychological make-up, and doesn't need to unravel how and why things occur. Such enquiries are superfluous to the survival of the human animal.

Instead, such enquiries are a sub-category of overall human meaning making that occur at the essence level. Ultimately, they emanate from the spiritual self, whose intent is always to strive to understand what is happening during the course of its existence. Hence all attempts made to understand anything at the essence level actually reflect the higher spiritual self's innate drive to understand.

The second fundamental kind of enquiry is one in which your own core consciousness becomes the object of your enquiry. This involves turning your everyday awareness within and striving to connect it to your core consciousness. This happens by degrees over an extended period of time.

The field of the first kind of enquiry is external to the core consciousness and involves experimentation linked to intense thought. The field of the second kind of enquiry is internal, occurs within the core consciousness, and involves experimentation in the absence of thought. This second field of enquiry will be explored in *Mystical Spirituality*. So for the rest of this chapter we will focus on the first field and on the process of enquiring into what is, strictly speaking, external to the spiritual core consciousness.

ASKING THE RIGHT QUESTIONS

Human beings rarely think through anything in their life in a calm, focused and rational manner. Instead, as we have repeatedly stated, the usual human behaviour is to fall back on assumptions, most of which date back to childhood, or beyond. And, as we saw in the example of the discovery of cave paintings at Altamira, the problem with falling back onto assumptions is that they get in the way of achieving a proper understanding of received data.

However there is another issue that clouds any kind of enquiry, spiritual or otherwise. The issue is that people find it very difficult to ask the right questions about deep matters – and by right questions we mean questions that lead to clear and useful answers. In general, when people ask deep questions about their life it is at times when they are under duress. Perhaps a loved one is seriously injured or dies and they ask, "Why did this have to happen to them?" Or something terrible may have happened to them personally. Perhaps their hopes and dreams have been decimated, or nothing in life is going their way, no matter what they try. They then cry out to whatever power they address on these occasions and ask, "Why me?"

The problem is that such questions are asked while experiencing intense emotions such as depression, self-pity, resentment or fear, or when people are severely frustrated and feeling like a victim of forces beyond them. The result is that when they ask, "Why did that happen to so-and-so?" or "Why me?", the questions themselves are certainly deep and serious. But they are not being asked in a serious way. Instead, what these people are really doing is venting. To clarify: At such times people are not asking a question to which they will subsequently seriously seek out the answer. Instead, they emotionally vent for a time, then when the intense emotional state passes they stop asking, "Why did that happen to so-and-so?" or "Why me?" and carry on with their lives.

In fact, if they seriously wished to find answers to their deep questions, the period when they should continue asking is precisely after those intense emotions have died away. Unfortunately, what usually happens is that when the churning emotion dies their deep questioning dies with it. They stop asking. And as a result they never do get an answer. Then at later times they lament how God doesn't understand them, or doesn't answer their prayers, or they become cynical and assert that life has no meaning, or that there is no God and existence is pointless. The key to finding deep answers to deep questions is that they need to be asked in the right way. When asked in the right way deep questions become serious spiritual questions. And spiritual answers will then certainly be found.

For example, if someone close to you dies, you could wonder in a general sense as to whether or not human beings reincarnate. Of course, this requires you to put aside all your conditioned assumptions regarding reincarnation, whether in favour or against, in order to initiate an open enquiry. An openly pursued enquiry will then lead to other related "how" questions: If reincarnation occurs, what is the mechanism? How does the spirit become re-embedded in a body? And how does spiritual identity connect with everyday awareness centred in the physical brain?

Then there are the related "what" questions: What does anyone bring into this life from the previous life or from the spiritual realm? What did that person bring in that influenced their life to follow the course it did? What have I brought in that influences my life journey? What am I doing here anyway? What is my purpose? What am I?

If enquiring individuals were able to put aside their assumptions and ask this series of questions seriously, in an open and focused manner, and if they were able to sustain their enquiry over a sufficiently long period of time to receive answers, they would not only reach a high level of understanding regarding the nature and purpose of their existence, but they would also likely progress towards achieving their major life goals, of which they would have become aware.

However, and as a caveat, it must also be noted that human beings rarely ask deep questions when their life is going well. They rarely seriously ask "Why me?" as they sit in a favoured holiday destination, eating fine food between taking dips in refreshing water. They rarely ask, "What is happening in my life?" when good fortune smiles on them or when daily life goes along "swimmingly". It is only in moments of misery and pain, when the texture of their life is punctured, that the deep questions tend to be asked. And, as we observed, they are usually a form of venting, being asked in a woe-is-me manner without truly serious consideration or follow through.

What this means is that, in fact, people do ask the right questions from time to time. The problem is that they don't ask them in the right way. And so they don't arrive at useful answers that they can use to understand and transform their existence. Let's consider the right way to ask questions.

ASKING QUESTIONS IN THE RIGHT WAY

No question exists in a void. Every question has a context within which it is being asked. This context needs to be considered, because assumptions will undoubtedly be present. For example, you could ask why a particular person no longer loves you as he or she once did. The context for this question is within a relationship. This relationship previously involved a particular intensity of emotion. Now the intensity of emotion has fallen. So something has changed. The question is, what? And why? And what should be done in response?

In any relationship, assumptions are present that may be sourced in each individual's psychological make-up. One of those involved might assume that she is a lovable person and so now be bewildered as to why she is not loved as she feels she deserves to be. Or the other might have an underlying and barely repressed fear that he will always be rejected in the end. So he has self-defensively and quite unconsciously withdrawn his emotional engagement in order not to be hurt. Naturally, this has diminished his input into the relationship.

In this situation the wrong way to ask "Why me?" is entirely emotionally, in a state of feeling sorry for yourself. Another wrong way to ask is while you are attacking the other person for changing their level of commitment. This will certainly drive a resolution to the situation, whether that be to end the relationship or to recommit to it. But demanding a resolution won't help either of the two achieve a deep understanding of what is going on between them. So even if both individuals recommit to the relationship, if they don't understand what is happening between them at a deep level, then that recommitment will effectively only paper over the cracks. And the emotional fissure will assuredly open again, and wider, at a later date.

The right way to enquire into the state of this relationship is to begin by examining the emotional context. This involves each looking at and admitting to what they want while also appreciating what the other person wants. Furthermore, this "want" needs to be at a deeper level than the superficial "I want you to love me". It needs to be at a level where the assumptions that underpin their emotional state, including their desires, fears, and even holes left by trauma in the fabric of their emotions, are uncovered.

Of course, uncovering deep emotional assumptions is very difficult. The most powerful and far-reaching psychological assumptions were conditioned into your psychological makeup when you were a child. Many of them involve painful, perhaps traumatic, events. During your childhood and teen years you coped with painful or traumatic experiences by covering them up. As a result they are now deeply buried. Exposing them to the light of day involves re-experiencing the original raw emotion all over again. The point of burying them in the first place was to avoid experiencing those emotions. Exposing them to the light of the everyday awareness inevitably involves reliving those same emotions to a greater or lesser degree. And everyone has an aversion to doing that.

Yet it is only by, first, recognising and admitting to those emotions, second, coming to understand where they came from, and third, working to eliminate them from your psychology, that you have the possibility of removing the buried emotions and attitudes that you have long assumed to be the case and that are now negatively affecting your relationship.

It is possible to do this type of emotional clearing without help, by yourself. Once you are familiar with the process, and provided you are able to cope with the pain associated with releasing deeply buried emotions, then you can certainly satisfactorily work through a considerable number of hidden and repressed emotional attitudes and behaviours on your own.

However, when first starting on this process most people need help from others. That may involve using friends as sounding boards to talk things over. It may involve attending group meetings where emotional clearing work is conducted. Or it may require seeking out a therapist and using an experienced advisor to get the self-enquiry process under way. Each individual must weigh up for themselves the type and level of support they wish to draw on, and decide for themselves what level of assistance is appropriate.

To complete this example, it is also possible that one or both individuals involved may use their enquiry into what has happened in their relationship to achieve new spiritual level understanding. This understanding could involve insights into emotional attitudes that were formed during former lives and that are now negatively impacting on the current relationship. It might involve insights into a relationship the two individuals had in a previous life. Or it may involve the two achieving deep and direct spirit-to-spirit communication irrespective of prior life connection. All these outcomes are possible. That is, if one or both sustain a serious enquiry into what is occurring.

This is an example of asking questions in the right way. Yet how does this relate to using new data to ask fruitful questions? Or, looking further back in the text, to treating beliefs as propositions? Answering these requires us to further explore what is involved in asking questions in the right way.

THREE STEPS TO ASKING THE RIGHT QUESTIONS

To enquire into the above relationship in the right way, a fundamental requirement is that one or both individuals are motivated to achieve a resolution. And they need to sustain that motivation until resolution is found.

If they remain wallowing in a woe-is-me reaction, or if they are locked into a blame game, or if an agreement is made to bury the feelings and continue, then the relationship may stagger on, but it is difficult, in fact almost impossible, to address and resolve the issues at the heart of the issue.

What is required to initiate a successful enquiry involves three steps: stepping back and observing, weighing the data, and formulating the question.

Stepping back and observing. First, you need to step back from your own feelings. This is often difficult. But without being able to distance yourself from what you feel and think you will not have sufficient inner space to observe and weigh up what is going on within you.

To explain this on the practical psychological level, what stepping back involves is using the intellectual or moving capacities of the essence self to observe the emotion-saturated behaviours of the socialised and biological selves. In this case of appraising a troubled relationship, the essence self's emotional capacity is not used to observe the situation because it is likely caught up in the socialised self's reactions. Instead, those parts of the essence self that are not directly caught up are most effective for observing the emotional behaviour, with an eye to identifying ingrained beliefs, assumptions, attitudes, repeated words, types of defensive behaviour, and so on.

Weighing the data. The second step is to collate these observations and treat them as new data, using it to think about yourself as if you were observing yourself from outside. This is an important point. You need to feel like you are observing yourself from another's perspective. But, of course, you have a privileged position, because you are closer to yourself than anyone else. And so you can perceive things, whether psychologically within in you or in your past, that no one else has access to. You can see things up close and personal. But you don't take anything you perceive personally.

It could be said that the first phase of stepping back involves seeing yourself in the right way. This second phase involves thinking about yourself in the right way. This is achieved by setting aside all assumptions, whether they be psychological, religious, scientific, or whatever, along with all defensive reactions. But to do this you need to become aware of what those assumptions are – because you can't detach yourself from thinking or from attitudes or from behaviour that you don't even know are there, or that you don't perceive as feeding your everyday awareness.

How do you expose and observe unrecognised assumptions? How do you come to recognise beliefs that are impacting on your feelings, thoughts, words and choices? This is where external insights provide useful data. It involves seeking insights from other people who have dealt with the same or similar situations. Valid insights may be communicated via lectures, books, study and discussion groups, or as a result of friends' observations or expert tuition.

External input is often required because during the initial stages of spiritual enquiry it is very difficult to recognise your own assumptions. It is a little like trying to stare at your own retina. You perceive the world through your assumed beliefs in the same way that you look using your retina. Just as the retina is part of the architecture of seeing, so assumed beliefs are part of the architecture of processing what you see. So getting helpful observations from external sources, or drawing on others' insights into the beliefs and psychological assumptions that power your outlook, are useful for helping you learn how to step outside them. What these external insights provide are observations about yourself that are objective. Objective observations are essence level observations of your socialised and biological selves. They may be made either by your or by others.

Formulating the question. By the end of the second step you have new information about your behaviour, attitudes and/or beliefs are that is not tainted by subjective feelings or buried under layers of self-defensiveness. Having first stepped aside from yourself by exposing your socialised self to the eye of the essence self, and having then gathered insights into your own biological and socialised assumptions, you are now in a position to take the third step and ask in the right way. That is, in a way that will lead to greater understanding.

In the context of the relationship, let's say the newly gathered data includes the observation: "I constantly feel I'm unworthy. I'm in a relationship with a man whose positive qualities far outweigh his few negative points. But I constantly feel like he's going to find someone much better than I am, someone much more worthy of his love, and that he's going to leave me."

Using this data (which is so much clearer and more precise than the previous plaint of "Why me?"), exact questions can now be asked. Questions such as: Where does my feeling of unworthiness come from? What fear underpins that feeling? Does he really think I am unworthy of his love? Or am I projecting my feelings?

This is how assumptions can be turned into propositions, which then may be used to initiate an enquiry. In this case, the assumption is that one is unworthy. That assumption is then turned into a proposition, "I constantly feel that I'm unworthy", and that proposition is used as an entry to enquire into what underlies the relationship.

The end result of asking the right questions is that one arrives at an understanding of the full context of the situation. In this case, the woman will arrive at an understanding of key aspects of her conditioning and of the repressed fear that drives her. She will then appreciate what the actual issue is. And be in an informed position to decide on the best way to address the situation.

To reiterate: First you step back and observe the situation. Next you collect data on what is happening within your layered self. If necessary you use insights offered by others in order to obtain an objective view of your behaviour, objective in the sense it is untainted by subjectivity or by self-defensiveness. Finally, you use the collected data to ask new questions that are informed by the fresh data you have obtained. These result is that deep questions are asked in the right way. Of course, this is neither an easy nor a quick process. Time, effort and dedication is required to see it through. And for that you need to be motivated.

USING MOTIVATION

As we stated earlier in this chapter, intention manifests from the spiritual self. In each life the spiritual self has planned to achieve certain goals, to address certain issues, and to meet up with and engage certain people.

In this sense, what you are striving to achieve in this life has been intended by you at the level of your own spiritual identity prior to your birth in your current body. At the level of the essence self, intent is deflected into motivation, because it is at the essence level that goals are identified and pursued, life issues are grappled with, and people are met and interactions occur. But in order to achieve these things the individual involved has to be motivated at the essence level to pursue them. And the plain fact is that not everyone is equally motivated.

Many things distract individuals during their life. They might find other goals, issues and people that attract them more than those the spiritual self has selected. They may get depressed, throw up their hands in despair, and stop trying. This happens to many people at some period during their life. They may become cynical about everything and everyone, including themselves, and undermine the opportunities that arise. In this last situation, cynicism is a defensive strategy that is adopted in order to avoid fully exploring life opportunities. Whatever the particular circumstances, many individuals end up losing motivation and so depart from their spiritual self's intent.

To return yet again to the example of the relationship, if that relationship was part of the spiritual self's intended life activities, then the spiritual self would urge the essence self to engage in the right questions and resolve the problems. This urge will be experienced as essence level motivation.

But if the relationship was peripheral to what the spiritual self intended for this life, then there would be much less motivation at the essence level to resolve the situation.

Of course, the situation is not quite this simple, because it could be that the relationship is peripheral to the spiritual self's intent, yet it may also be the case that resolving feelings of unworthiness is central to that intent. And so the spiritual self may motivate the individual to use this unplanned and peripheral relationship to address the central life issue of unworthiness. Such is the way that the spiritual identity utilises accidental life opportunities to motivate the essence level self and so achieve its intended aims.

One of the arts of living a fulfilling life is identifying deep-seated goals and sustaining one's motivation to achieve them. In this sense there is a direct correlation between motivation and fulfilment. Being able to sustain motivation results when one aligns one's essence level identity with the intention of the spiritual self. And a sense of deep fulfilment occurs when essence level identity achieves what was intended at the spiritual level. We will discuss this is greater detail in *Practical Spirituality*.

CONCLUSION

The purpose of this chapter is to indicate the degree to which beliefs about the world and assumptions you make about yourself may be used as springboards to arrive at deeper understanding. We also want to make clear the fact that your beliefs and assumptions are what hold you back from appreciating the much wider context in which your spiritual self plays out. Not only does your individual identity contain multiple layers, of much of which you remain completely unaware, but you yourself may be making decisions outside the perception of your everyday awareness.

Some of these decisions occur at the subconscious level, in the basements of your biological, socialised and essence selves, and involve your repressed feelings, attitudes and fears pushing you to make a particular choice, or alternatively to avoid making a decision. Others occur at the supra-conscious level, in the spiritual self, and involve feelings, concepts and goals of which you are also, at best, barely aware.

Historically, human beings have had all kinds of beliefs about these subconscious and supra-conscious impulses. Repressed attitudes and fears that suddenly bubbled up into everyday awareness and caused mayhem to the individual and those nearby used to be labelled the work of the Devil. Insights that appeared as spontaneous visions or in dreams were once labelled the work of angels or saints. In recent times the scientistically-inclined have sought to reduce all such phenomena to the gurgling of chemicals and the flashing of electrical impulses within the nervous system and its brain.

The plain truth is that the layered self is much richer than these simplistic explanations allow. And in the end it doesn't matter what you initially did or did not believe about your own self. What matters is what you discover. And the understanding that you derive from your discoveries.

CHAPTER 11

Achieving Understanding

ACHIEVING UNDERSTANDING depends, first, on where you start from and, second, on how you progress from there. If you start mired in your assumptions and beliefs, and you have no pragmatic process for evaluating either them or your life experiences, then you are not going to arrive at any understanding of great depth during your life.

On the other hand, if you are willing to stand aside from your nearest and dearest beliefs, and if you remain motivated to dig into both your experiences and how you process and respond to your experiences, then we can guarantee that the sky is certainly not the limit. Why? Because in the end there is only one crucial element in achieving understanding. That crucial element is you.

If you "turn up" in your life and make full use of the opportunities presented, then at the death of your body, when you conclude your life journey, you will be in much better shape than when you began. Of this there is no doubt. And by "better shape" we refer to your level of knowledge and understanding, not to having a good-looking corpse.

As we stated in the previous chapter, ask the right questions in the right way and the right answers will follow – right answers in the sense not of what you want to hear, but in the sense of what you need to hear and learn from in order to evolve as a spiritual being. To this degree we assert that spirituality does not hinge on agreeing with or rejecting shared beliefs. It doesn't hinge on whether you are a manifestly good person or a manifestly bad person. It certainly doesn't hinge on having God's approval. Spirituality, for you as an individual, hinges on the reality of what you are as a spiritual being and on your engagement with yourself as that being. Your engagement, carried out in a serious manner – and being serious does not preclude having fun – will enable you to achieve understanding, given that achieving understanding involves growing from immaturity to maturity, even to achieving mastery.

THE FOUNDATIONS FOR UNDERSTANDING

Understanding is achieved as a result of processing the knowledge that you draw out of your experiences. But before you can achieve understanding you need to develop insight. And before you can develop insight you need knowledge. And, as we have said, in order to obtain knowledge you need to challenge what you think you know. We'll return to the example of the relationship to explain how this occurs.

The starting point is that both partners experience dissatisfaction. Let's say one partner vents about the situation, becoming immersed in anger, self-pity, resentment, sadness, or any of the many emotions human beings feel when life does not go how they wish. As a result the observations this partner makes are coloured by his negative emotional reactions. Accordingly, he draws no detached knowledge from his observations. And deep insights are out of the question. Over time his seething emotions likely calm down, but he won't have come to any understanding about what has occurred. And those tensions and fears that disrupted the relationship from his perspective remain unresolved.

In contrast, let's say the other partner makes a serious attempt to get to the bottom of what is going wrong. She makes a number of pertinent observations drawn from interactions. Those observations provide knowledge of her own psychological makeup and perhaps that of her partner. This knowledge then provides insights into what is happening. These insights, extrapolated from knowledge obtained via observation, may, for example, be regarding the impact of her own upbringing or the particular form of fear that is negatively impacting on the relationship. Depending on their depth, such insights offer a means of understanding what makes her tick psychologically. And, perhaps, what makes her partner tick also.

Of course, if the issues involved are deeply buried, or if they are fed by multiple factors on both sides, it may take years to unravel and fully understand the situation psychologically. And, naturally, in order to continue the investigative process for that long, sustained motivation is required.

It is the need to sustain motivation where most individuals stumble. When a relationship is flagging, rather than dig into it, it is much easier to change the centre of attention by re-focusing one's life away from the relationship and onto something else, such as work, or children, or an enjoyable hobby. Alternatively, one may make a decision to end the relationship. Or to shift emotional focus onto someone else. Choosing any of these options doesn't preclude understanding what went wrong. But most people prefer distraction to getting to work with a spade and shovelling ordure.

As we stated at the start of Chapter Nine, the initial stages of grappling with any issue tends to be unappetising. Few wish to get the hands dirty with ordure. And, to be fair, it is not for everyone to grapple with their errors while they are living through them. Some only review them years later, during their retirement years, when they have the distance and leisure to review the mistakes in their life. Most wait until after their body has died, and the journey is over, before reviewing key issues in their life.

On the other hand, if anyone genuinely and seriously enters into the issues that beset them while or soon after they occur, whether those issues be emotional, intellectual or practical, they take a huge step towards leaving the stable and setting out on a path that leads up the mountainside.

BECOMING SAVVY

The way we are defining it here, knowledge derives from the data one gathers as a result of observing what is occurring in one's life. Insight results when you extrapolate back from that knowledge to appreciate causes, or when you apply the knowledge to some practical purpose. In the case of seeking to resolve the problems derailing the relationship, insight is used to comprehend what is going on psychologically. This involves developing insight into defensive behaviours that were shaped in childhood and that influence adult behaviour.

In general parlance, having insight is known as being savvy. Being savvy is applied to all spheres of human activity. A sportswoman tries out plays during training, is given feedback by trainers and coaches or makes personal observations, and from this process becomes savvy regarding how to play.

However, being savvy doesn't automatically translate into understanding. Perhaps only later, after reviewing what was experienced and observed during the training session, is it possible to develop understanding of why that play was practised, how the play fits into the game plan, and how the player fits into that play. Of course, many sports people have great savvy on the field, which enables them to perform their role extremely well during the game. But they don't have understanding regarding the game plan from the coaches' perspective. This is a situation in which being game savvy gets them by perfectly well. But the next step of developing understanding involves obtaining a higher level perspective than savvy involvement facilitates.

We have previously said that knowledge is hard won. The same applies to becoming savvy and to developing understanding. They are stages in the same process, the end result of which is to gain mastery in a particular field of human endeavour. Naturally, mastery is not just theoretical but is applied practically during the course of daily life.

Becoming savvy is also dependent on what part of the layered self is involved in the process. In the above sports example, it is the essence self that becomes savvy, using observations gained while playing. It is also the essence self that develops higher level understanding.

However, it is frequently the case that individuals become savvy in their socialised self. In this situation they become sufficiently perceptive to observe others' behaviour, and they use their observations to whatever end is consciously or unconsciously determined by their socialised self. Being savvy, especially where others are not, is often used to defend a position at work, or to take down others who might challenge that position. At other times savvy is used to make money or to manipulate others. The motormouth salesman is a classic example of the individual who has sufficient savvy to push the "buy now" buttons of potential purchasers and so manipulate them to make a sale. Cunning is also a manifestation of socialised savvy, as is projected guilt that one individual deploys on another to get what he or she desires.

Naturally, such low-grade savvy does not match the quality of insights that are obtained as a result of serious questioning. Nor can it lead to essence-level practical, emotional or intellectual understanding.

ESSENCE UNDERSTANDING AND SPIRITUALITY

The understanding that individuals achieve during the course of their life occurs at the level of the essence self. But because the essence self embodies the goals of the spiritual identity, that essence level understanding actually directly feeds the evolution of that identity. As this relationship between spiritual self and essence self is not widely appreciated, we will briefly comment on essence, spirit and understanding. These preliminary comments will be expanded in later books in this series.

As we have already pointed out, prior to being born each spiritual identity plans in lesser or greater detail what it wishes to achieve in its upcoming life. This includes setting goals, deciding on which psychological issues it desires to work through, and selecting essence traits, social environment and bodily characteristics. Of course, not all plans work out in the way that is intended. Social environments can change in unanticipated ways, accidents happen which affect opportunities, and unplanned or unanticipated choices may be made that may radically change a life's direction.

Nonetheless, whatever happens offers opportunities for a spiritual identity to experience human life via its selected sub-identity. And everything it experiences provides occasions for the sub-identity to learn and grow.

As we have made clear, it is the essence self that does the learning and growing – that is, should the individual decide to engage seriously with his or her life situations. The result of seriously engaging with a particular situation is that understanding is achieved. And this understanding contributes to a life lesson being learned. Some lessons are small, some accumulate one on top of another, some are profound. Yet whether large or small, each equally contributes to the growth of that sub-identity during the course of its life.

At the end of the life, when the body dies and the sub-identity dissolves, what has been experienced and learned (negative and self-inhibiting as well as positive and self-nurturing) is uploaded to the spiritual identity, which then appraises what lessons have been learned or not learned. Some of what the spiritual identity "chews on" post-life was planned and the lessons went along the lines of what was aimed at. Other experiences pan out quite differently to what was anticipated, being richer or leaner or just different. And other experiences are completely unanticipated. Just the same, each provides an opportunity to learn from.

This combination of planned and accidental experiences is usually what happens when a spirit enters the human domain. The grandest plans can be undone by a spur-of-the-moment decision. As a result, a life can spin off in a completely unforeseen direction. And that is as it should be. No one is keeping score. No one gives anyone else a mark for what they do or do not achieve. A life is what is experienced irrespective of plans. Each individual has choice not only prior to incarnation, but also every minute of every day during the course of that life. That many individuals are too inhibited to fully exercise that choice, for both positive and negative reasons, is another issue.

The upshot of all this is that the essence level understanding achieved during any life has some elements that fit with the goals of the ongoing spiritual identity and some elements that are tangential to those goals. Yet they all equally contribute to enriching the identity and feeding its ongoing evolution. And evolution, however it comes about, is the purpose of experiencing both the embodied and non-embodied realms.

ACCUMULATING LIFE LESSONS AND UNDERSTANDING

We began this chapter by emphasising the need to acquire understanding. We further indicated that understanding develops out of possessing and using insight, otherwise known as being savvy. And we suggested that being savvy depends on utilising knowledge derived from observing yourself and others in life situations. We have concluded that understanding results when life lessons are learned. And the entire process contributes to the growth of the essence self, which in turn contributes to the evolution of the ongoing spiritual identity.

This process is repeated life after life. If prior to being born you organised a situation in order to learn a particular lesson, and you get diverted by some other experience and so learn a different lesson, no matter. Nothing is lost. In a subsequent life you will again have the opportunity to work through what you planned to but didn't. And not necessarily in the very next life.

We are aware that in stating this, and in various other comments we have made in earlier pages, we have been reinforcing a reincarnational view of human existence that could be viewed as an assumption we are making rather than a fully explained fact of human existence. This is unavoidable, because spiritual identities living in a body have cramped perception. And what is obvious to the non-embodied is far from obvious to the embodied. Ultimately, either you are prepared to process this information or you are not. Again, that is completely up to you to decide.

However, the point with which we will conclude this chapter is that individuals do not just achieve understanding in relation to single aspects of human existence. Rather, understanding accumulates and is carried by the spiritual identity from life to life. In the same sense, the process of maturing not only occurs in the context of each life, but maturity also grows as experiences accumulate from one life to the next and as life lessons are drawn from each.

Wise individuals who attain to mastery at being human do so not by luck but because they have worked at it life after life. In this sense everything you do contributes to what you become. And we recommend that as a concept well worth you striving to understand!

CHAPTER 12

Each Life
Is An Experiment

T HERE IS A WIDESPREAD assumption that most individuals have an experimental period in their lives, usually during their teenage years, when they experiment with lifestyle, sex, relationships, drugs. Sometimes, years later, when a marriage or relationship falls apart, or when losing their job initiates a radical change in lifestyle, individuals enter a second adult period of experimentation.

However, these periods of experimentation are usually haphazard, without planning. During these periods people know what they want to try out, but rather than planning what to experience they tend to put themselves into a situation where what they want to explore is likely to happen, whether that be meeting certain sorts of people, getting into a particular profession, having sex, taking drugs, and so on. Then, when an opportunity arises, they jump in boots and all. That is not the type of experimentation being advocated here.

We would call jumping in boots and all an *experiential* approach to life. In contrast, an *experimental* approach to life involves the much more orderly questioning of beliefs and assumptions, gathering new observational data related to them, and using that data to delve into what you think you know. Furthermore, what is explored is never random. Even when individuals jump into experiences that seem to occur by chance, such experiences are rarely encountered entirely randomly, and are never actually entered into by chance. They are always chosen at some level within the layered self.

We realise this last statement is contentious. Many people are convinced that life is random. They assume that human beings are born into a certain family and culture by chance, that accident of birth offers certain social opportunities and not others, and that conditioning largely shapes a person's psychology and dictates how individuals respond to their environment. They further assume that an individual identity is wholly extinguished when its body dies. All this leads them to conclude that a life's constituent factors are a random combination. And, because death extinguishes everything anyway, ultimately an individual's life experiences do not add up to anything of significance outside the life itself. Some of the scientistically inclined go so far as to claim that existence as a whole has no purpose or point.

The remainder of this chapter is a response to that outlook. We do so by outlining what human existence looks like from the spiritual domain.

HOW RANDOM IS HUMAN EXISTENCE?

From the spiritual perspective each life, each incursion by spirit into the physical realm, each occasion when a spirit enters a body and its associated social environment and experiences a human life, is an experiment. An experiment in what? An experiment in consciousness.

Each life is an experiment in which certain very specific parameters are set in place prior to birth. And the experiment is to discover what the spiritual identity, experiencing the human domain from within that body, makes of the opportunity. From this perspective, each life is an experiment in which an ongoing spiritual identity explores a particular aspect of human existence in order to evolve its own consciousness – given that whatever the spiritual identity experiences, processes and learns during the course of each life goes back to its ongoing spiritual identity, becoming material that feeds its ongoing evolution.

In simple terms, being embodied is an opportunity for you to develop your abilities, to expand your awareness of what is occurring in the world around you, to extend your awareness of what is happening in depth within you, and to achieve knowledge, insight and understanding of as many facets of human existence as you choose to explore. This knowledge, insight and understanding is what feeds you at the spiritual level and what contributes to your evolution as a fragment of spiritual consciousness.

As with most complex experiments, while a greater or fewer number of outcomes are planned prior to an individual spirit's incarnation, before the spirit enters the foetus, an individual life's outcome is never set in stone. Sometimes, when a spiritual identity reviews a life after its completion, that life is disappointing to the spirit. It is disappointing because conditions set in place prior to the spirit being born were not explored to the extent that was sought. Pre-organised opportunities were not taken. However, at other times expectations are exceeded, because more insight and understanding is achieved than was anticipated.

Of course, the experiment which is a life is not the same as, say, a chemical experiment. In chemistry one chooses particular chemicals, already knowing what their properties are, then combines them, also in a known way. If heat and duration are maintained as planned the outcome can be very accurately predicted before the actual experiment has taken place. This is not what happens with a life. The outcome of a life is almost never completely what was anticipated. Indeed, a sizeable percentage of lives do not end up at all resembling what was anticipated prior to embodiment.

Why is this? Why do lives depart from what was planned? The answer is that in a chemical reaction only a small number of factors are involved. Furthermore, they interact according to fixed relationships and laws, and so outcomes can be reasonably predicted. In contrast, a human life journey involves innumerable factors. While there are certainly probabilities regarding how an individual will act, once chance is added to life circumstances the possible outcomes become so complex that how an individual will respond even to pre-organised opportunities cannot be accurately predicted.

Yet this lack of predictability is not a negative. It is just how it is. It is what makes each and every life journey an experiment. An experiment in experiencing, processing, responding, learning and growing.

One way of thinking about this is to imagine a hundred flower seeds being planted in various parts of a garden. When they bloom each will look slightly different due to having grown in different soil and having experienced different levels of sun and water. There may also be differences at a genetic level, with one seed more fully adapting to the garden environment than another. So slight variations in soil, sunlight, water, genetic make-up and adaptation result in flowers that are very similar but not identical. These differences may be viewed as random if the seeds were scattered around the garden randomly. But what if a gardener deliberately planted seeds in different soil beds throughout the garden, and also consciously varied the amount of water and sunlight received by seeds in different parts of each bed? Then the garden becomes an experiment in horticulture. The experiment's result depends on what is being tested for. For example, the gardener may be experimenting to ascertain what soil is best for certain seeds, and what optimal levels of water and sunlight are best suited to seeds growing in a particular soil.

To a visitor who doesn't have all this information it may seem that the gardener has done a poor job, because some flowers are decidedly bigger, brighter and healthier than others. Such a visitor may even think that this variation among the flowers affirms his assumption that life is random. Because, to his perception, here is clearly a random set of growth outcomes.

But, in fact, the gardener has planned it all. The apparently random results are the outcome of an orderly experiment. And so the visitor, through lack of information, is merely projecting his own assumption onto what he perceives. If he was able to see more deeply he would perceive that what is apparently random is actually a manifestation of order.

This same process, on a far larger scale, also applies to human existence. Billions of fragments of spiritual consciousness have been seeded into billions of bodies, which themselves are planted in the soils of different physical and social environments, and fed differing kinds and intensities of inputs. As a consequence, each spirit undergoes different types and combinations of experiences during the course of each life. Some of these experiences are chosen. Some occur by accident, just because the individual happened to be there when an event such as a car crash occurred. And some are the result of uncontrolled natural forces, such as hurricanes or floods.

Some individuals live for a brief period, others for a century. Some live in traumatic environments, others live placid lives. Some intensely explore very specific areas of human activity and develop expertise, even mastery, in those areas. Others make little effort. Yet others are thwarted from day one, and either end up frustrated and embittered or learn acceptance and to go with the flow. Some make one mistake and pay for it for the rest of their life.

Others live charmed lives, and seem to escape all consequences of the various scrapes they get themselves and others into. And, of course, whatever is
experienced is processed by an everyday awareness in which very particular
psychological traits predominate. So the ways different individuals perceive,
process and respond to the same experiences, let alone to different experiences, varies enormously.

This is why human experience is so richly nuanced. And why human
existence is not random. And yet neither are outcomes fixed.

HOW RANDOM IS AN INDIVIDUAL LIFE?

The extent to which a single human life may be called an experiment is
determined by the extent to which certain pre-conditions have been set in
place, the aim being to discover how that spiritual identity copes with those
circumstances and uses them to navigate through life.

We deliberately use the term *navigate* here because, while a life's pre-
conditions are determined, once the life journey begins it is over to the individual to navigate through and around the various obstacles, opportunities
and distractions that it meets. The end result of a life is not adjudged a success
or failure on the basis of what it achieved externally, although some lives certainly do have a physical outcome as their goal. Rather success and failure are
adjudged on the basis of what was experienced, what was learned from those
experiences, and the extent to which the individual used all that to evolve.

Life outcomes are always interesting, no matter whether they adhere
closely to the life plan or depart wildly from it. A scientist may set up an
experiment and, once the results are in, exclaim, "I didn't expect that to happen!" Yet he may actually be pleased because the unexpected result has
opened up a whole new field of research. Similarly, on reviewing a just-lived
life, an individual spirit may see that little panned out as expected, yet what
was experienced and learned has opened whole new possibilities for future
experimentation.

In all this we need to make clear that there is no big scientist in the sky
who is experimenting with your embodiment in the human domain. Rather,
it is you yourself who is both the subject of the experiment and who is doing

the experimenting. This is why we say that becoming embodied as a human being is an experiment in consciousness. Life after life you are testing yourself in human existence and using the opportunity to hone your everyday awareness. The experiment in incarnation is completed when you have learned to love selflessly and when you have gained mastery over the experience of being a spiritual consciousness living in a body, to the extent that your spiritual consciousness is actively present within your everyday awareness.

Along the way, while experiencing and learning life after life, each individual spiritual identity gets to develop a range of skills, abilities and talents, to the degree of mastery if it so chooses. Again, there is nothing pre-ordained by anyone or anything external to the individual concerned in any of this. It is all up to what the individual wishes to do and how hard they push themselves. Because, at the end of a cycle of incarnations, it is definitely the case that some individuals end up knowing and understanding more than the norm, while others learn and understand less. And that difference is entirely due to the effort made by each individual fragment of spiritual consciousness.

While the human domain may be viewed as a vast field of interlinked experiments in consciousness, there is no "big scientist" mixing a little of this, a bit of that, shaking it all up, applying pressure, and seeing what results. Rather every one of the billions currently living on the planet Earth are using the conditions of human existence to experiment on themselves in order to evolve.

To reiterate, nothing is pre-determined. On the planetary scale, humanity is free to explore the myriad available choices and to nurture or poison local environments, to wipe out other species, or even to wipe out a significant proportion of its own population.

So the human experiment, on the scales of both large populations and the individual, is open-ended. What is chosen today has a direct impact on the opportunities available tomorrow. And what choice is made from tomorrow's opportunities determines what opportunities are available the day after that. And what is chosen from those opportunities closes down some opportunities that were available while simultaneously opening up others. And so on.

Of course, we are talking not only of days but also of lives. From the very moment when you stop reading this text there are branches of possibilities.

Once you choose one branch, and walk a little way down it, other branches of possibilities appear. Some branches take you back towards where you were, others take you further away. The choices you make (and not making a choice is making a choice), and the experiences that result from those choices, then shape the journey you make in this life, and subsequently, life after life.

LIFE IS NEITHER RANDOM NOR PRE-DETERMINED

While there are certainly elements of chance in human existence, an individual human life is not random. And neither is it pre-ordained. No aspect of your life certain is guaranteed to play out in a particular way. It might be pre-planned. But it is not pre-determined.

Why? Because each individual has choice, no matter how much or how little an individual exercises that choice. And while we have stated that a body and its social environment is chosen by a spiritual identity before it is born, and while plans are set up to maximise the benefit to the individual identity while living in that body (whatever the individual has determined that benefit to be), yet the individual can always choose not to follow the plan. Everyone is always free to branch off onto another line of exploration and to test themselves there. To this extent individuals may facilitate or sabotage their own best interests on any or all of the bodily, social, essence, energetic or spiritual levels. You have that choice.

People say that life is random. We have asserted that they do so because they are unable to perceive the underlying pattern. The scientistic view is that life is run entirely by objects that come into existence in accordance with pre-determined laws and that they interact by chance. Such individuals are missing much that is going on. They are projecting a fixed outlook onto existence and failing to perceive that which is not fixed.

Equally, the religious who say that God has determined everything are projecting their assumed beliefs onto life and seeing only what they allow themselves to see. This equally applies to those who say of a meeting or an incident, "That was meant to be." Plans are made. But choice always applies. And outcomes are never pre-determined.

The claims of both the scientist and the conservatively religious are overly simplistic. It could said that they are also both reductionist, in the sense that they seek to reduce the complex, marvellous and organically branching possibilities that constitute human existence to much less than they actually are. As we said, allowing fear to drive their everyday awareness leads them to reduce the complexity of life to simple assertions.

THE CHALLENGE IS TO OVERCOME FEAR

The fact is that everyone allows fear to stifle them at times. Sometimes fear arises in the middle of decision-making and dissuades an individual from making a beneficial choice. At other times fear is so overriding that it disrupts an entire life.

While we do not condone language that exploits the word *enemy*, if you wish to think of your existence as having an enemy, that enemy is fear. Fear stops people in their tracks. Fear leads individuals to run away from the one thing they came into this life to embrace. Fear pushes people to betray their friends and to sabotage themselves. All the many negative emotions and attitudes that plague human existence, all the negativities that taint and poison a life journey, have their source in fear. A divergence from one's life plan that occurs as a result of curiosity may turn into an interesting, scary, entertaining or educational surprise. A divergence from one's life plan made because of fear is a wasted opportunity.

Despite our asserting this, there is nothing to be fearful of with respect to your life choices. There are no mistakes in life. Everything, whether chosen after deliberation or on the spur of the moment without thought, offers an opportunity to experience, to learn and to grow. So there is no need to fear taking a misstep. There is also no need to feel guilty or to view yourself as a failure. Or, equally, to sustain a self-inflated sense of yourself as privileged or entitled or special.

Life is ultimately about making the most of whatever opportunity comes your way, and exploring that opportunity without fear and in a self-aware and loving manner. Do this each day and, whatever path your journey takes, your life in the human realm will prove fulfilling and satisfying.

TWO CHALLENGES

CHAPTER 13

Discover Something
New About Your Self

T O BRING THIS BOOK to a close we wish to offer two challenges to you, our reader. These challenges are designed to consolidate the concepts that have been presented in the foregoing pages. They will also provide you with material about yourself that will be helpful when you embark on the task of reading the second book in this series. That is, of course, should you choose to continue reading these missives from another place located beyond time. It is actually a place you already know, but that you are naturally cut off from during the course of living a human existence.

Every life comes with its particular positives and limitations. The positives promote inner growth, the limitations inhibit growth. Both sets of conditions are self-selected by each spiritual identity before it is born. However, what is not often appreciated is that both sets are useful, not just the positive. Indeed, it could be said that limiting factors are more useful because they become obstacles that have to be overcome. And in the act of overcoming them individuals learn not only more about themselves, in depth, back to their childhood, and perhaps beyond, but in having to grapple with and overcome limiting factors they develop the positive inner qualities that take them, one step at a time, towards becoming a more loving and knowing spiritual identity.

Of course, because you are a spiritual identity, you were already more loving and knowing in your non-embodied form, when you were preparing to reincarnate, than in your incarnated form. But being loving and knowing is much easier to sustain while non-embodied than while embodied. The reason for this is that embodiment unavoidably brings with it numerous limiting factors that impinge on the spiritual consciousness residing at the core of a human identity. We earlier used the metaphor of the Augean stables full of ordure and observed that they need to be cleaned out. In fact, human existence frequently feels much of the time like you are wading through ordure. And this is an apt feeling, because the state of embodiment, compared to your non-embodied existence, is a state of limitation.

As we also commented earlier, the human everyday awareness is highly complex in comparison to those of other species on the planet. But when compared to the state of consciousness of a non-embodied spiritual identity, the human everyday awareness is unavoidably narrow and highly selective. And so, for a spirit residing within a body, the state of being embodied necessarily generates a feeling of limitation.

From the spiritual perspective, all your feelings of frustration, of loss, of unhappiness, of despair, of being hemmed in and unable to fully express yourself, may be tracked back to the simple fact that you are a broad-visioned spiritual identity "trapped" within the limiting apparatus of the human body, its brain and its associated social identity. Of course, you are "trapped" by your own volition. And you have chosen embodiment in order to hone your ability to enter any aspect of reality and retain control of your chosen vehicle. Self-control is reflected by the degree to which you are able to acquire knowledge and at the same time, with equanimity, manifest selfless love, no matter what is happening around you and to you.

In this sense, the aim of taking on the experiment of human embodiment may be described as mastering the art of incarnation to the degree that you may become a knowing, insightful, understanding and loving human being. This is all you have to accomplish as a spiritual identity embodied in the human domain – and we are well aware of the difficulty of achieving the task that we blithely encapsulated in the words "all you have to accomplish", because we have gone through the process ourselves. We know in excruciating detail the joys and the costs of human embodiment. We also know that honing your spiritual consciousness in the fires of human embodiment is a richly rewarding experience.

Naturally, you cannot know this, because you are immersed within the mid to late stages of the cycle of human migratory incarnation. This is a truth that we have discovered through experience, which may take you many more lives to confirm for yourself. But we offer it so you may know that no matter how tough your life becomes, it all has a purpose. It all contributes to your personal spiritual evolution. It all leads to higher and greater experiences. Do not doubt this.

This brings us to the first challenge we wish to make to you, a challenge that we offer in order that you may take another step up the mountainside towards the peak that is the goal of human incarnation.

STAGE ONE: GATHERING OBSERVATIONAL DATA

The first challenge is with respect to what you assume, know, or think you know, about yourself. Everyone has questionable modes of behaviour, the worst of which are usually the most hidden. This is because they arise from the greatest trauma. There is a need to eventually excavate these deeply buried trauma. But we do not advise beginning there. It is much preferable to begin with beliefs, assumptions and behaviours that are less deeply ingrained and therefore are much more easily accessed.

The purpose of this challenge is for you to recognise a limitation within you, to own up to it, and to trace it back to its origins. Origins may involve a particular event or set of repeated circumstances. All limitations certainly hinge on a fear. So recognising the fear that underpins a particular limitation is a significant start in the task of exploring the layered self.

To start you need to identify a limitation. This is equivalent to the scientist's task of gathering preliminary data. In order to gather preliminary data on yourself we suggest you engage in one or more of the following:

- Make a note of a criticism a family member or friend makes of your actions, words or attitudes. It may be a repeated criticism. Or it may be a one-off comment. Get to grips with the criticism. If need be ask the others to clarify what they mean. Ask them for other instances when they observed you repeating the actions, words or attitude.
- Or: Make a note of an action, words, attitude or situation that you engineered that you are not proud of, that you are uncomfortable

with, or that makes you feel ashamed. Dredge your memory for other similar occasions when you did the same thing. If you think it would be useful, ask others for their observations of you doing those things, if you consider that will provide further material.

In order to gather this material effectively, you must not argue with whoever you ask. You must not engage in the defensive behaviours of denying, justifying, deflecting or attacking. Accept what you ask for in silence. And write down what you remember and what others offer so you have a record and it remains frsh and clear in your mind.

Some care needs to be taken when you ask others for their observations. This is because what you are seeking involves recalling negative behaviours and feelings, and different people react very differently to being reminded of these behaviours. The challenge for you is to dig into them and be reminded of times when you were less than a loving and knowing human being. The challenge in extracting information from others you have been negative towards is that they may not appreciate being reminded of what you did to them. Or of the negative emotional reaction they reactively manifested towards you. Or of the sense of limitation such an occasion stirred within them.

So be very careful how you go about obtaining observations from others. The point of this challenge is to obtain observational data on yourself. It is not for you to upset others by making them feel they are being confronted or being required to relive an experience they found distasteful. Accordingly, a useful way to begin could be to ask third parties for their views on your behaviour, third parties being observers rather than directly involved.

Next collect a second set of data as follows:

- Repeat the same data gathering exercise with respect to what makes you feel happiest. In particular, identify activities that made you happiest when you were a child. These are activities that came naturally to you, likely needing little encouragement from others, or that as soon as you saw the opportunity to engage with them that you jumped into "boots and all". Looking back to your childhood is useful because during adulthood work and raising children require you to engage in all kinds of activities that you may well enjoy, but they are not necessarily activities that generate in you an all-encompassing feeling of happiness and bliss. Again, make a list.

STAGE TWO: OWNING UP TO THE DATA

Having gathered the initial observational data, the next stage is to make sense of it. And especially to use it to gain insight into your psychological makeup. When you recognise these behaviours are a consistent part of what you do, not necessarily on a daily basis, but that are certainly repeated over time, then you are in a position to "own them" and to acknowledge them as being present within your psychological make-up.

The first step in making sense of the observational data is to identify patterns. Pattern recognition involves not just recognising that the behaviour is repeated, but appreciating the context in which the behaviour occurs. For example, let's say that the observational data relates to moments of anger. Let's say this anger flares up suddenly, but only occasionally, perhaps unexpectedly, and that it burns with an intensity that is usually out of proportion to the situation in which it occurs. In seeking to appreciate pattern and context, answer the following questions:

- Do these incidents of anger (or whatever is being examined) occur only with certain people? i.e. with both parents, with father or mother only, with particular siblings, when dealing with bosses, are directed only towards men, only towards men when you are with a certain third person, only towards women, or a woman, or only when another emotion such as frustration or despair is present?
- Do these incidents of anger occur only in certain situations? i.e. at work, when driving, when dealing with people close to you, when there are constraints such as a time limit, when you are being pressured to perform, when you feel you are being ignored, or used?
- Do these incidents remain in play for some time? i.e. do not flare up and die away quickly, but instead the anger remains bubbling within for some time after the actual incident that stimulated it is over and done with? Observe what thoughts and feelings swirl around with

the anger. If the anger then flares again shortly after, what circumstance leads to that occurring? What activities of self-calming follow the anger, such as taking it out on family, eating, engaging in physical exercise, etc.

It needs to be noted that negative emotions such as anger, self-pity or guilt often flare up while drinking alcohol. This is not because alcohol stimulates the anger, but that a certain degree of drunkenness (a degree that differs from person to person) short-circuits the socialised self that normally inhibits or suppresses the expression of the negative emotion. So the negativity is always there, lurking in the depths of the psychological make-up, but it only manifests when the socialised self's guard is down. In this sense, it could be said that alcohol is a useful tool in revealing suppressed emotions and attitudes and so may be used as an aid in self-analysis. However, please note that we are not advocating the practice of drunkenness as a spiritual discipline!

What is being sought in stage two is a more specific appreciation of what is happening, particularly of the emotional context. So all related emotions, behaviours and commonly stated words, along with the conditions to give rise to the negative emotion, also need to be noted and added to what has been observed during stage one.

For the alternative form of this challenge, with respect to the observational data on happiness, carry out the same exercise as above, but this time seeking to contextualise your deepest feelings of happiness or bliss. Identify whether other people are involved, whether these are the same people all the time, or whether different people are involved, but who perform the same role in relation to what you are doing. Or is it something you prefer carrying out by yourself?

The information we are suggesting you ferret out is tricky to describe because it is easily confused with more superficial forms of happiness. We are attempting to push you to recognise deep level feelings of happiness or bliss. An example of the difference between shallow and deep is that many people engage in activities that they enjoy immensely, such as gardening, or cleaning, or cooking. These are activities they do by themselves and they enjoy it so much because it offers an opportunity to escape the constant noise of home life or the hassles of working with others. But what is actually being enjoyed is the peace and quiet rather than the gardening, cleaning or cooking, however satisfying those activities may be.

It is also the case that some forms of experience may be highly enjoyable and satisfying to you at certain stages of your life. For example, sports may wholly engage a teenager. Another teen may be equally enthused by drama, or by fashion, or by politics. The question is, is this enthusiasm and the deep satisfaction generated by engaging in this activity sustained into adulthood? Does it continue through the years? If the answer is yes, this is the kind of happiness and bliss we are suggesting you investigate. If the answer is no, then some other bliss is likely to animate you.

However, a caveat must be made here. Sometimes an event occurs in early adulthood, such as work or marriage or parenthood or financial crashes or any other similarly life-impacting event, that takes an individual away from engaging in their bliss. If you feel that there is something from your childhood that you need to return to, or something that you have unfinished business with, it may indicate an activity that generates bliss. Equally, it may indicate something else altogether. Discernment is always required when investigating these nebulous aspects of human experiencing. Of course, everyone has moments when they are deliriously happy. What we challenged you to discover in stage one is a repeated activity that gives you the greatest feeling of satisfaction and bliss. In stage two we are challenging you to discover the context in which that activity is, or has been, carried out.

To summarise: Getting away from others does not constitute what we are referring to here. Truly blissful experiences are felt at a deep level, to the degree that you are likely unable to fully articulate what you experience. This is the type of experience we are suggesting you seek out.

STAGE THREE: IDENTIFYING FEAR OR BLISS

By now you will have gathered considerable data, all based in observation, that collectively forms a small body of knowledge about yourself. The next stage is to dig into this body of knowledge and gain insights into what motivates you.

The body of knowledge around a limiting factor, such as anger, is driven by a particular fear. It may be fear of missing out. Or of being ignored. Of not getting your way. Of being rejected. Of being hurt. Of being inadequate to the task at hand. There are many varieties of fear that drive the human psychology. We will look at them in greater detail in the next two books in this series.

For now it is sufficient to ask you to dig into your anger, or resentment, or self-pity, or your lack of ability to complete tasks, or whatever limiting belief, attitude or behaviour you are investigating, and to see if you can discern the particular type of fear that drives it. Each fear itself has echoes in formative childhood experiences, and beyond. Being sufficiently open to consider what this fear might be, even if you are unable to nail it decisively, is a significant step in lifting your feet out of the ordure and beginning the journey up the mountainside.

The same applies to digging into the activity that makes you happiest. Underlying this activity is a particular form of bliss. Just as a particular fear drives your limiting behaviours, so there is a particular form of bliss that drives you to continually engage with certain activities. Because varieties of bliss are much less part of common parlance than are forms of fear, we will name the most fundamental forms of bliss, as experienced in the human domain. These are: The bliss of serving the good. The bliss of creating. The bliss of taking on challenges. The bliss of achieving understanding. The bliss of serving an ideal. The bliss of communicating. And the bliss of commanding.

Tracing your deepest happiness back to one of these forms of bliss will provide you with a valuable insight into what drives you in your life. We will expand on the nature of bliss in the next book, *Practical Spirituality*.

CONCLUSION

This dual challenge, of digging into one aspect of your existence that is limiting and another aspect that generates deep happiness, will provide you with an understanding, on the one hand, of what holds you back in your spiritual journey and, on the other hand, of what is worth pursuing because it provides the most satisfaction.

Of course, there are always limiting factors in your life, both external and internal, that hold you back from exploring your bliss. These limiting factors need to be overcome. And in overcoming them you learn more about yourself and you strengthen your ability to pursue your bliss. In this way limitations and positive qualities work hand-in-hand to help you progress in your evolution as a spiritual identity.

What is the nature of this identity? How may it be identified by you living an embodied existence? This brings us to the second challenge.

CHAPTER 14

Explore Your Inward Spiritual Sense

A T THE START OF THIS BOOK we used the phrase "personal spiritual sense". We now return to that idea and re-present it to you in the form of a challenge. We asserted, as our second premise, that every human being has a spiritual consciousness at their core, that each individual consists of a spiritual self residing within a body.

This spiritual self is what generates in you complex meanings about the world, meanings that exceed the basic demands of the animal drives of eating, defending territory, reproducing, nurturing the young and surviving. Your search for great love, your efforts to understand, your nurturing of others outside your gene pool, your drive to produce great things, to share all you have, and to become a better human being, each emanate from your spiritual self.

In the first premise we suggested that assumptions drive human existence. So everyone either assumes that this spiritual self exists or they assume it does not. There is, and can be, little rational debate over this between those who accept this proposition and those who do not. This is because the assumption exists at a deeper level than the functioning of either the faith-filled emotions or the rational denying intellect.

The existence of the spiritual self is assumed to exist, or is assumed not to exist. But neither position is based in observational data from which you may gather knowledge regarding the existence of your own spiritual self. We assert that all assumptions, whether for or against the spiritual self's existence, are insufficient. What is required is knowledge.

How may knowledge of the existence of the spiritual self be gathered? This is what this challenge is designed to help you achieve.

THE EVIDENCE IN HUMAN CULTURE

In Chapter Three we made the point that much in human culture far exceeds what is required to sustain humanity's animal existence. We additionally observed that this excess to animal need actually derives from the drive of the spiritual self as it explores the physical and social environments into which it has been born, as it strives to understand what is happening underneath the surface phenomena of its daily existence, and as it loves often altruistically and with a generosity that far exceeds what is strictly required to survive as a species.

The scientistically inclined would reduce the richness and altruism of human culture to genes struggling to survive, to bodily chemicals gurgling, to brain-embedded electrical impulses flashing, and to the survival mechanism that is the body strutting. Those who are conservatively religiously inclined would seek to ignore much of this richness, and even to suppress aspects of it, on the grounds that it is immoral, blasphemous, or ignores or denies God's existence. Their disapproval flows out of their view that much in human existence is inharmonious with their particular concept of God – to which we add there have been innumerable God concepts thorughout history, as there continue to be today.

We submit that both the scientistic and conserbative religious views are myopic. Indeed, both are assumed perspectives that ignore what is blatantly and obviously present. There is a commonly repeated phrase, used when reviewing information or evidence that is clearly present, that people are ignoring the elephant in the room. People get so bound up in details, and so focused on relating those details to their assumed beliefs, that they fail to notice what is most obvious about what is being examined.

The debate over climate change is one example in which the elephant in the room of human activity is ignored by many. So is the debate over peak oil being passed and what the impact on the biosphere will be if fossil fuels continue to provide humanity's primarily energy source. We have already discussed fear as the driver of defensive behaviours, so won't retread that ground here.

The point we are making is that the richness, complexity and intricacy of human achievement, the sheer bravado of what some individuals attempt, and manage to pull off, the èlan with which they approach their goals, and the admiration and applause others direct their way when they succeed, are all manifestations of the spiritual self's drive to make the most of the opportunity provided by human embodiment. That this is actually so simple and obvious is what makes it so difficult to perceive. To support this statement, we offer three levels of evidence.

THE EVIDENCE IN RELIGIONS AND SCIENCES

The sciences and the world's many religions have one clear thing in common: they are both manifestations of the spiritual self's drive to get beyond the surface of life and to dig deeper into what is occurring.

In the case of religion, the mysteries of birth and death, the issue of what guides human destiny, the need to comprehend why certain things happen and others do not, especially momentous natural events such as disasters or plagues disrupt human existence relate to God, and why some individuals are sensitively endowed beyond the norm, are all manifestations of the spiritual self's attempt to make sense of its existence in the human domain and to relate it to what it considers to be a higher spiritual dimension.

As we stated at the very beginning of this book, religions are a mixed bag, with correct and incorrect concepts, nurturing and repressing doctrines, and much that is just plain silly, all sitting together. Yet this does not invalidate the fundamental value of all religions, which is that they provide a socially approved forum for the spiritual self to appreciate and commune with its fundamental realm, that being the spiritual domain.

Similarly, the sciences are a socially maintained apparatus by which enquiring spirits may come to grips with where they live on this planet, the nature of biological existence, what reality is constituted of, and how that reality may be manipulated. As with religions, false assumptions fuel the sciences, notably the scientistic tendency to which we have already drawn attention. But this does not invalidate the driver that underpins the sciences, which is to seek deep knowledge about the world and universe and to delve into what lies beyond everyday sense perceptions.

Both religions and the sciences are manifestations of human culture. It could simply be said that religions seek to show people how to love, while the sciences provide an opportunity to know. This is only partially correct, of course, because many knowledgeable people function within the world's religions, and a love of humanity, even of the planet as a whole, drives many in the sciences to seek new discoveries that will benefit all.

Nonetheless, it may broadly be stated that religion is about love and the sciences are about knowledge. And love and knowledge in all their many forms, in whatever context they flower, and even when mixed with elements that limit their full flowering, are evidence of the spiritual self in action.

THE EVIDENCE PROVIDED BY ANOMALOUS DATA

Everyone has had an experience that falls into the general category of the spooky. It may be that you have seen a dead family member or friend, or at least have become aware of their presence. Or you have had a premonition about something happening that has indeed come to pass. Or you have felt inexplicably attracted to another person. Or, equally inexplicably, repelled by them. You may have felt that you wanted a particular thing to happen, and it did happen. Or you may suddenly decide you should talk to someone, and soon after that the phone rang, or you bumped into them somewhere, or they knocked at the door.

As we stated earlier, the religious, at least in Western nations, officially avoid "spooky stuff", putting it down to the occult, of which they disapprove. However, many of the serving clergy are personally much more open to the spooky side of existence, because in their pastoral care they come face to face with it on a regular basis, particularly when ministering to the dying.

Similarly, in the sciences spooky stuff is usually put down to chance events, to hallucination, or to projected wish-fulfillment. This is because of the scientistic tendency to either dismiss anomalous data, which is data that doesn't fit with their worldview, or to explain it away on the basis that physics or chemistry can account for everything. Accordingly, at the official level, scientists are trained to disregard the spooky side of human existence. However, as with individual clergy, individual scientists are not as dismissive.

As a result, considerable data has been gathered by scientists regarding reincarnation, out of body experiences, near death experiences, along with investigations of ESP, vivid dreaming and other non-ordinary forms of perception. This data is widely available in printed form for all those who wish to learn more about such matters. Hence, observations of phenomena, as well as personal experiences, that fall outside the normal and everyday, attest to the fact that more is going on in the human domain than can be strictly accounted for on purely materialist and rational grounds.

We submit that some, although certainly not all, of such anomalous occurrences are expressions of the human spiritual domain impinging on and overlapping with the human physical domain.

THE CHALLENGE: FEEL YOUR OWN SPIRITUAL SELF

Having presented easily accessed cultural evidence that the spiritual self manifests universally within human activity, and having then drawn attention to the "spooky stuff" that equally attests to the ways that the spiritual dimension is present within human daily existence, we now shift to the third and final category of human spiritual experience we intend to touch on here, that being evidence of the personal spiritual self.

The best way to obtain confirmation that not only does the spiritual domain overlap with the human realm, but that you exist as a spiritual core consciousness within a body, is to gain direct awareness, within your everyday awareness, of your spiritual self. Of course, this is more easily said than done, because many people naturally erect barriers that prevent them from contacting their own spiritual self. Others explain away what is actually a spiritual experience by ascribing it to other causes. It is also the case that many people don't have sufficient information to appreciate that an experience is spiritual in nature when it occurs. So they put it down to being "one of those things". Or they dismiss a subtle impression, feeling or thought as imagined.

We admit it certainly does take time to gain direct experiential knowledge of the presence and nature of your spiritual self. Moreover, there are no shortcuts to achieving this knowledge. Nonetheless, we challenge you to try this exercise as a way of at least feeling the presence of your own spiritual self.

Start the exercise by choosing a quiet place to sit. Sit in a way you are accustomed to and comfortable with. Close your eyes. Now sense yourself sitting inside your body. Hold this sensation for ten seconds. Next imagine that you are situated a few feet above and behind your seated body, looking down at the back of your own head. You can either visualise the back and top of your head and shoulders, or just hold a feeling that your body is below your awareness and slightly forwards. Hold this image or feeling for a further ten seconds. Now go back to sensing yourself sitting in your body. Hold this for another ten seconds, then shift to looking down at your body, from above and behind, again for ten seconds. For as long as you feel like doing so, shift between the two perspectives of being seated in your body and looking down at or being aware of your body sitting.

To help you shift from one perspective to the other, you might find it useful to take an extra large breath in when you shift from being seated in your body to looking down at the back of your head. And you can expel an extra large breath as you descend or "slump" back into your body. There is no need to hold your breath between the large inhale and large exhale. Breath normally between. To perform this part of the exercise it is necessary to give your attention to each perspective. Not following inner chatter is also required. After a period, open your eyes.

Now sense yourself sitting in your body, looking out at whatever is around you. Try to feel yourself looking out through your body's eyes. Feel yourself as being separate from what is looking. A very subtle feeling is now being sought. So subtle it is easy to think that you are imagining it.

What we are asking you to do is somewhat like being in profile to a mirror, then turning very quickly towards the mirror and catching a glimpse of your own profile. Another metaphor that suggests the same experience is that of trying to look at the back of your eyeballs.

Physically, both are an impossibility, of course. But the idea behind them offers a hint of what we are asking you to notice: that you are looking out using your everyday awareness, but at the same time you can feel within or beyond that awareness something much deeper that is looking at you looking out.

CONCLUSION

Obtaining a taste of your own spiritual self is actually quite common, especially for those who are in the mid to late stages of the cycle of incarnation. It is all part of the process of maturing as a spiritual being who is experimenting with its own capabilities during the course of living in the human domain. In the following books in this series we will provide other means for you to access your spiritual self and to deliberately and consciously bring it into the purview of your everyday awareness.

For now, if the exercise does not present you with either a direct feeling of or suggest the presence of your spiritual self, we challenge you to process the evidence provided by human culture, by the activities of the sciences and the religions, and by anomalous experiential data, and to use it to appreciate the spiritual self's presence in the human domain.

With that we bring to a close this introduction to a twenty-first century experimental approach to exploring human spiritual nature.

Afterword:
On This Channelled Book

F OR THOSE UNFAMILIAR with channelled literature, which is the genre this book falls into, and who wonder at how this work was produced, we note the following. The process of channelling adopted here has involved placing thoughts into the mind of our scribe, Keith Hill. There are advantages and disadvantages to disseminating information from the spiritual domain into the human world in this way.

The advantage in this particular case is that we have been able to connect with a nimble mind that has dedicated itself to expressing as accurately and as succinctly as it is able concepts that are not only deep, but that occasionally veer towards what is nigh on impenetrable – that is, as far as the unprepared reader is concerned. There is no easy way to explain some of the deeper aspects of spirituality. So dealing with a mind that enjoys, indeed positively enthuses over, the task of organising complex material and presenting it in more easily digested bite-sized chunks is a decided advantage to us, given that our goal in these books is to express the arcane in digestible form.

The disadvantage is that we can only use the "ingredients" that already exist within our scribe's mind. It is difficult for us to introduce completely new concepts, because there is no frame of reference for our scribe's mind to make sense of what we project. Therefore, when we wish to make a point that is outside our scribe's existing frame of reference we have to use concepts that are already known to him. We have to re-arrange the "available ingredients", so to speak, in order to present a sequence of ideas that simultaneously makes sense within the context of our scribe's mind and that accurately expresses what we wish to convey.

Despite this disadvantage, we acknowledge the effort our scribe has made to prepare himself and to make himself not just a willing, but a decidedly able, vehicle for what we are sharing. Part of that preparation involved years of study of a wide range of spiritual, philosophic, scientific and cultural texts. He also had to learn to make contact with us. And he has had to learn to stay out of the way during the process of writing, neither censoring, editing, rejecting nor unnecessarily elaborating on the thoughts we project into his mind. This is no easily achieved task. Accordingly, we acknowledge and thank him for his willingness to take on the role of scribe.

We must add that this is not a one-way exchange. Our scribe has himself pondered deeply on the matters that are presented in this series of books. He has grappled with terminology, sought to link disparate concepts from a range of different historical and contemporary spiritual teachings, and he has consistently sought to clarify just what those concepts and teachings mean to him personally, in the context of his own spiritual search.

The result is that the mind we have to work with has available a range of ideas, perceptions, conceptual frameworks and ways of looking and thinking that together have given us considerable flexibility in presenting an approach that is suited to today's Western-educated, English-speaking enquirer into the arcane territory of things spiritual.

We also wish to acknowledge the potential readers of these books. In order to draw value from what is offered in these pages, you also have had to prepare yourself. You have had to work to bring yourself up to the level of reading and processing sufficient to suck the nectar from what we present. We say "nectar" because it is not the actual words that offer spiritual savour, but what is conveyed via the words. Yet in stating this we are very aware that what is written in this book, as well as in those that will follow, makes for very intense reading, and that many readers will certainly find this nectar is not to their taste.

This response is not necessarily a slight on potential readers' abilities, because their nature may be more suited to other forms of delivery. This is as it should be, because a wide variety of texts, written in many languages, and from a wide range of perspectives, has been produced throughout history to satisfy the requirements of those living in different cultures and who possess various psycho-spiritual make-ups. On the other hand, the difficulty may result from laziness. Or from an inability to do what we suggest in the second chapter, which is to set aside assumptions, at least for the period of reading, in order to savour what is on offer.

Nonetheless, it must be admitted that this text, and the four books that follow, are predominantly transferred via our scribe's intellect. This has resulted in the nectar offered here being a rich concoction. Given the intensity of delivery, we accordingly advise all readers to read slowly. Certainly gulp down any or all books first time round, if that appeals to you. But then go back and read chapter by chapter, even one section at a time.

This is because while we have no desire to tax readers unnecessarily, neither do we wish readers to rush over material that it has taken our scribe years to digest, and that, despite his and our shared desire to make what is complex and difficult clear and straightforward, in many places certainly demands close and sustained attention. One of the principal truths of reality, that applies to all conscious beings wherever they exist, is stated in the homily, "You get out what you put in." That is certainly the case here.

We commend you for being adventurous. And may that adventurousness enable you to knowingly enjoy the full smorgasbord of experiences that human embodiment encompasses!

Glossary

Aura	A field of multi-coloured luminous and radiant energy around a person or object. The human aura functions as a channel of communication between those in the spiritual domain and the embodied spiritual identity.
Act of guidance	A spiritual level initiative to communicate with an embodied being. This initiative may be through the stimulation of an idea, by a fleeting or persistent internally visualised image, by apparent internal thought or speech formation, by a sensation, by psychokinesis (such as bringing one's attention to a useful book by pushing it off a shelf), and so on.
Beliefs	Beliefs of all kinds are naturally generated by the human everyday awareness. There are innocuous beliefs, such as that an apple a day will keep the doctor away, beliefs that involve practical necessities, such as that a light will turn on when you flick the light switch, and beliefs that reflect true knowledge about the world, such as that the Earth orbits the Sun. This last form of belief is best described as knowledge. All beliefs remain unverified assumptions until they have been tested and it is seen whether or not they reflect reality. Validated beliefs become the basis of new knowledge. The growth from a child level identity to a mature identity is reflected in the journey from merely believing to actually knowing. A set of untested beliefs

forms a credo. Both religious believers and those who advocate a scientistic outlook promulgate credos. Psychologically, a problem with beliefs and credos is that believers invest their everyday identity in what they believe. So any questioning of their beliefs is interpreted as a threat to their identity. As a result, individuals self-defensively reject ideas and data that contradict their beliefs. What they then learn during the course of their life is limited and their growth is stymied.

Biological self Commonly known as the body, the biological self is grounded in the human animal, homo sapiens sapiens. The biological self's physical traits are shaped by genetic inheritance. It also contains and sustains the human sensory and nervous systems, along with the brain and its cognitive functions that process perceptions and so underpin everyday awareness.

Essence self The higher level functions of the human animal, characterised here as consisting of the moving, emotional and intellectual functions. The essence self is where the growth of human abilities and identity occurs.

Energetic self More commonly known as the aura, this is the energetic envelope that surrounds the body, on average approximately two and a half meters from the body's skin. See *Aura*.

Everyday awareness In ordinary terms, the level of awareness manifested by the alert human brain. In the terms designated here, everyday awareness is a function of the active parts of the biological, socialised and essence selves. One of the aims of embodiment is to imbue the everyday awareness with the intent and awareness of the spiritual self.

Everyday identity The identity each individual maintains during the course of daily living. Everyday identity naturally changes as an individual grows from infant to child to teen to adult. Some aspects of everyday identity are projected onto an individual by others, other aspects are constructed by the

individual him or herself in response to life situations. Psychological impositions and trauma significantly influence
the nature of everyday awareness. *See Identity, Sub-identity* and *Fear.*

Experimental spirituality An approach to spirituality that treats beliefs and
assumptions not as truths but as propositions that one
needs to enquire into. This approach also involves perceiving your life as an experiment in consciousness, with
you being the experimenter, using your own life to experience, learn and evolve as a spiritual identity.

Evolution   The spiritual self evolves as a result of experiencing, processing experiences, extracting life lessons, using what is
learned to transform the five-layered self, and both the
five-layered self and the spiritual self growing as a result.

Devil   A projection of human fear.

Fear   There are two fundamental sources of fear. The first is the
existential fear a new and naive spiritual identity feels on
first being embodied in the human domain and it is unable
to control the body in which it dwells. The second level is
the fear emanating from the old brain, an animal defense
mechanism that manifests as flight or flight. This animal
fear has been socialised over the eons and now manifests
in subtle behaviours. As a result fear has become embedded in human culture, fuelling numerous religious beliefs.
A variety of different socialised fears drive the psychological make-up of everyday identity. These fears include
the fear of being vulnerable, of being inadequate, of not
having enough, of losing control, of missing out, of being
worthless and of the new. Each individual psychological
make-up is driven by one of these fears. That particular
fear is usually selected prior to incarnation, but is reinforced during childhood experiences. Self-calming and
defensive behaviours are used to cover up fear, which then
becomes deeply buried within the socialised self. As such,

fear fuels all the factors that limit an individual's ability to make the most of opportunities. Fear limits growth. One's underlying fears needs to be addressed in order to facilitate inner growth.

Five-layered self   A model that proposes the human self consists of five layers: the biological self, the socialised self, the essence self, the energetic self and the spiritual self.

God   The universe was created. This creator may be called God, if one wishes to use that designation. However, this creator is not a person or personal in any way a human being can understand. The human everyday awareness is simply incapable of comprehending the nature of the vast all that is, let alone the nature of the even vaster creator of all that is. *See Imagined deity.*

Imagined deity   A projection onto reality by the human everyday awareness, a process by which the incomprehensible creator of all that is is reduced to human dimensions. A typical form of imagined deity is when the creator is reduced to the human bodily dimensions of Jesus, Krishna or of a "super person" of some similar kind. As such, imagined deity is a projection of human wish fulfilment, in which human beings imagine an extra-natural father-like being cares for them personally. They certainly are cared for, but it is by spiritual beings who, out of love, have taken on the task of nurturing the embodied. The creator is not directly involved.

Identity   Identity exists on many levels. External identity consists of bodily and socially constructed identity. Internal identity consists of the self-image one constructs for oneself. Essence level identity consists of practical, emotional and intellectual abilities and expertise. Everyday identity is the identity people project and protect during daily interactions. Underlying them all is spiritual identity, the ongoing identity that uses external, internal, essence and everyday identity to live a human existence. *See Everyday identity* and *Sub-identity*.

Insights   Insights are obtained as a result of enquiring into what one observes. Psychologically, insights involve either appreciating how a particular emotion, attitude or behaviour came to be conditioned into one's make-up, or how they are expressed in a variety of different situations in daily life.

Intention   Intention emanates from the spiritual self. All spiritual identities intend to use the experiences gained during their incarnation in a human body to learn, to transform their functioning at all levels of their layered self, to grow, and to evolve as a spiritual being.

Knowledge   Information obtained via direct perception, that has been processed and verified. Verification may occur as a result of repeated observations, and also via peer review, in which group members compare their experiences and conclusions. Knowledge is a tool to vanquish fear. *See Beliefs* and *Insights*.

Life plan   A plan shaped by a spiritual identity prior to its incarnation in a body. Incarnated individuals have the choice to keep to a life plan or to abandon it during the course of any life journey. Part of the experiment that is incarnation is to see how the identity copes with what it has organised for itself to experience and learn during that life. Lives that abandon a life plan are not failed experiments. They are merely alternative experiments, and have equal value, because all experiences provide life lessons and so may feed an individual's evolution. Abandoned life plans are usually taken up again in a subsequent incarnation.

Love   Love exists on multiple levels. There is the biological love of parents for offspring. There is the mutually dependent love mixed with sexual attraction depicted in stories of romance. And there is the altruistic love of an individual for others who are not part of his or her direct gene pool. The highest form of love is spiritual love, called agapé.

Agapé has no projected desire other than goodwill. When embodied individuals experience agapé emanating from high level spiritual sources, it invariably invokes a state of serene peacefulness and contentment.

Mastery

The end result of a series of life lessons. Mastery is gained in any aspect of human endeavour as a result of sustained application, in which one focuses attention on a limited range of experiences, develops skills appropriate to that context, learns from mistakes, and by degrees gains expertise. Mastery is gained as a spiritual identity incarnated in a human body when one's everyday awareness is suffused by the spiritual self and when one has learned to become deeply knowing and perfectly loving.

Meaning

Meaning is constructed within the everyday awareness. Each species has its particular everyday awareness it uses to construct its own unique meanings from what it perceives. Hence flies construct fly meanings, dolphins construct dolphin meanings, eagles construct eagle meanings, and so on. Because the human everyday awareness is complex, it constructs complex human meanings. These meanings involve processing perceived events and giving them significance, striving to understand what caused those events, and ascribing purpose or purposelessness to those events. However, because ascriptions of significance, understanding and purpose (or not) occur within the everyday awareness, and because that awareness is limited, human meaning-making is intrinsically skewed and limited.

Meditation

A state of inner or dual awareness achieved by practising any one of various techniques involving internal or external focus. The body may be kept still or in rhythmic movement for the duration of the state. Differentiated from sleep by continuous mental alertness. Generally a prerequisite for spiritual awareness by those who are not naturally sensitive due to having insufficient lifetimes of experience.

Motivation   Intention emanating from the spiritual self manifests within the essence self as motivation. Motivation must be sustained at the essence level in order to carry out any task, whether spiritually oriented or everyday. Spiritual intention remains constant, but motivation is impacted by an individual's reactions to life experiences and so waxes and wanes.

Negativities   Consisting of negative emotions and attitudes, negativities are psychological obstacles that must be overcome in order for the layered self to function at its optimal level and to grow and evolve. Fear underpins all negativity.

Observation   Occurs when one part of the essence self observes another part of the self in operation in order to collect data. Typically, the intellect is used to observe one's own emotions in operation. Individuals often use their essence self's emotional centre to observe others' behaviour. This can offer useful, even correct, psychological insights. However, the problem of observing via the emotional centre is that judgement, or self-deprecation, or envy, or blame, or some other negative emotional attitude, is often embedded in the emotions. As a result valid observations become caught up in subjective emotional experiencing. To be useful, observations need to be carried out in a detached, non-judgemental way. This is why observing using the intellectual parts of either the intellectual or moving centre is preferred to using the emotional centre.

Original sin   An imaginary concept that is part of the socialised control/inhibition mechanism by which religions control believers and sustain their cultural status, and that believers use to inhibit themselves in the choices they make during the course of their life journey. Many individuals cling to the concept of original sin because it deflects their attention away from their own limitations and inadequacies, ascribing their deficiencies to a purely imagined anciently enacted situation.

Reincarnation Reincarnation is axiomatic to this experimental view of human existence. Spiritual identities choose to experience embodied human life in order to learn and grow. The cycle of incarnation is repeated until the spiritual identity learns what it came to learn, and grows in the ways it chooses. The cycle then comes to a close and the next phase of evolution is embarked on.

Scientific method An experimentally-oriented process used to obtain new knowledge about what happens in the world. When applied to spiritual practices it facilitates the acquisition of new knowledge that has been extracted from, and verified in, the context of personal experience.

Scientistic outlook A set of assumptions that underpin scientific enquiry. Includes the assumption that only matter exists, that there is no realm apart from or beyond the material world, that human consciousness is entirely a by-product of the biological and chemical processes of the body's central nervous system and its brain, that no non-material spiritual or supernatural entities exist, and that what cannot be explained in rational and naturalistic terms does not exist.

Self-calming A psychological mechanism that helps an upset everyday identity return to its normal inward state. Self-calming generally follows a shock of some kind in which fear is stirred up. Self-calming behaviours shift attention away from the upset and towards what is familiar. Self-calming behaviours vary between different people and depend on their psychological make-up, but may include eating, drinking, smoking, exercise, playing, shopping, violence or running away. Self-defensive behaviours are a form of self-calming.

Self-defensiveness Behaviours the everyday identity uses to cope with emotionally upsetting, confronting or invasive life situations.

Defensive behaviours are driven by fears of various kinds and manifest in denying, justifying, deflecting and attacking. The particular patterns of defensive behaviours present in an individual's psychological make-up are usually shaped during the childhood and teen years. They become crystallised at the onset of adulthood, if not earlier, and dictate how an individual defends his or her everyday identity in social situations.

Socialised Self   The socialised self consists of a psychological and behavioural layer within the five-layered self that is shaped by the social conditions into which an individual is born and develops. Language, education, family, social norms, work, opportunities, and so on all contribute to the formation of the socialised self. Where the biological self is shaped genetically, the socialised self is shaped by social and environmental conditioning and by the way the individual responds to that conditioning. As such, the socialised self is a social construct. Self-image is a function of the socialised self. The socialised self underpins everyday identity.

Spiritual self   Within the five layered self, the spiritual self is the individual's core spiritual consciousness. To itself, the spiritual self is a fragment of a larger spiritual identity. Its intent, wherever it is and whatever it is experiencing, is to learn and grow. Spiritual identity is not static. It evolves as it learns from its experiences. Its goal is always to become a more loving and knowing identity.

Sub-identity   In each life an ongoing spiritual identity enters a body and takes on the genetically inherited and psychologically conditioned characteristics that together form a unique human identity. This sub-identity exists for only the duration of that lifetime. Over the course of repeated incarnations each ongoing spiritual identity explores the human realm using a series of often very different sub-identities. At the end of its cycles of incarnations, a spiritual identity's experiences in the human domain consist of what it has experienced via its complete range of individual and unique sub-identities.

Transformation The spiritual self's intention in the human domain is to transform its five layered self. Life lessons feed inner transformation. And as the layered self is transformed, it grows. This growth in turn feeds the evolution of the ongoing spiritual identity.

Truth There are various kinds of truths. Assumed truths are inherited. They include conditioned beliefs and assumptions. When beliefs and assumptions are tested they lead to new knowledge that may be viewed as providing newly discovered truths. However, these are provisional truths. Provisional truths are truths that will do for now, but that will eventually be supplanted by new discoveries and even newer provisional truths. Those who consider they know The Truth are using what they think they know to hide behind. What they are driven by is an underlying fear.

Understanding Is achieved as a result of processing the knowledge drawn from life lessons. Because life lessons involve confronting one's own limitations and fears, knowledge is always hard won. When, during the course of everyday living, this hard won knowledge is applied to oneself and others, it is transformed into understanding. The understanding individuals extract from their experiences, during the course of their life, occurs at the level of the essence self. Knowledge is also extracted from experiences by the spiritual self, after a life is over and during the post-life review process. But that knowledge can only be claimed as understanding when it is embedded at the essence level during the course of living subsequent lives.

CPSIA information can be obtained
at www.ICGtesting.com
Printed in the USA
LVHW092356130723
752465LV00016B/164